Contents

Each page has a title telling you what it is about.

Instructions look like this. Always read these carefully before starting.

Read these word problems very carefully. Decide how you will work out the answers.

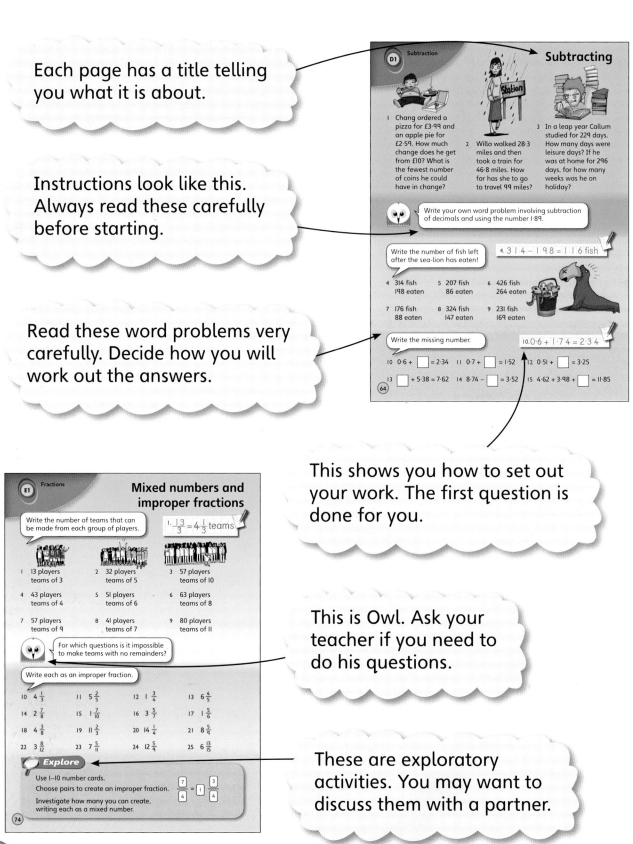

This shows you how to set out your work. The first question is done for you.

This is Owl. Ask your teacher if you need to do his questions.

These are exploratory activities. You may want to discuss them with a partner.

Multiplying by 10 and 100

Label the digits. Multiply by 100. Write the new value of the underlined digit.

1.	H	T	U					
	3	6	1	× 1 0 0 = 3 6 , 1 0 0				

Value = 3 0 thousand

1 3<u>6</u>1   2 45<u>2</u>   3 6<u>8</u>   4 7<u>1</u>6

5 <u>6</u>05   6 <u>4</u>24   7 28<u>1</u>   8 <u>3</u>48   9 9<u>9</u>9

10 1<u>1</u>0   11 1<u>9</u>3   12 9<u>1</u>   13 7<u>6</u>3

How many times must you multiply by 10 to get from 1 to 1 million?

Be a mathillionaire! Choose the correct answer. Write (a), (b), (c) or (d).

14 430 × 10 is:
   a) 43 000   b) 4303
   c) 430   d) 4300

15 7602 × 10 is:
   a) 76 020   b) 76 002
   c) 760 200   d) 7602

16 351 × 100 is:
   a) 35 001   b) 35 100
   c) 35 101   d) 351 000

17 8080 × 10 is:
   a) 808 080   b) 808 010
   c) 80 800   d) 808 008

18 5010 × 100 is:
   a) 501 000   b) 5010
   c) 50 100   d) 50 001

19 764 × 1000 is:
   a) 7640   b) 764 000
   c) 76 400   d) 76 060

1 Multiply each red number by 100. Find the blue number that matches your answer.

1. a and m

a) 3604   b) 288   c) 28 800   d) 36 060   e) 40 000

f) 5480   g) 501   h) 711 010   i) 63 700   j) 548 000

k) 490   l) 7111   m) 360 400   n) 4900   o) 50 100

p) 637   q) 3606   r) 360 600   s) 4000   t) 711 100

u) 400   v) 9090   w) 909 000   x) 49 000   y) 54 800

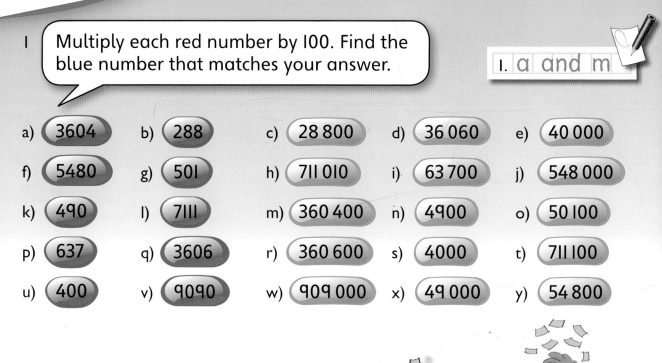

2 How many months are there in a century? In a millennium? How many weeks in a century? In a millennium?

3 A car costs 47p per mile to drive. How much does it cost to drive 100 miles? 1000 miles?

4 James saved £15 per week for 100 weeks. How much did he have? How much would he have after 2 years?

Copy and complete.

5. $273 \times 100 = 27,300$

5   273 × 100   6   3648 × 10   7   4875 × 10
8   314 × 1000   9   402 × 1000   10   7679 × 1000
11   5138 × 100   12   620 × 10   13   532 × 100

Start with a number, e.g. 7. You multiply it by 10. Your partner multiplies it by 100. How many more multiplications must you do than your partner to get over 6 million?

Multiplying by 10, 100 and 1000

Write the wages for doing each job 10 times.

1. £5·50 × 10 = £55

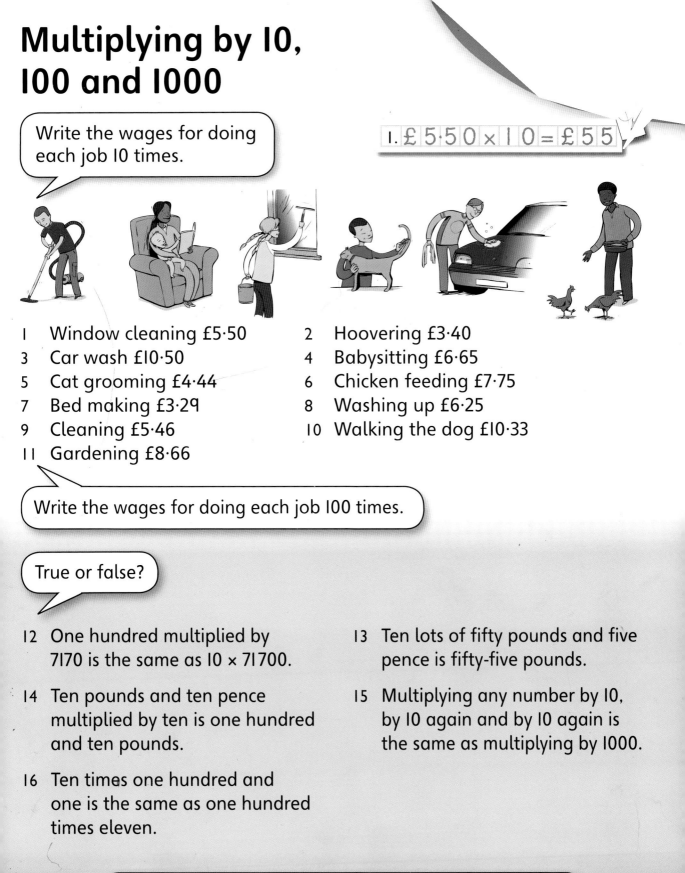

1 Window cleaning £5·50
2 Hoovering £3·40
3 Car wash £10·50
4 Babysitting £6·65
5 Cat grooming £4·44
6 Chicken feeding £7·75
7 Bed making £3·29
8 Washing up £6·25
9 Cleaning £5·46
10 Walking the dog £10·33
11 Gardening £8·66

Write the wages for doing each job 100 times.

True or false?

12 One hundred multiplied by 7170 is the same as 10 × 71700.

13 Ten lots of fifty pounds and five pence is fifty-five pounds.

14 Ten pounds and ten pence multiplied by ten is one hundred and ten pounds.

15 Multiplying any number by 10, by 10 again and by 10 again is the same as multiplying by 1000.

16 Ten times one hundred and one is the same as one hundred times eleven.

Start with £5·50. Multiply it by 10 five times. Talk with your partner about whether the total is going to be less than or more than £1 000 000. Now work it out!

5

Multiplying by 10, 100 and 1000

How many centimetres?

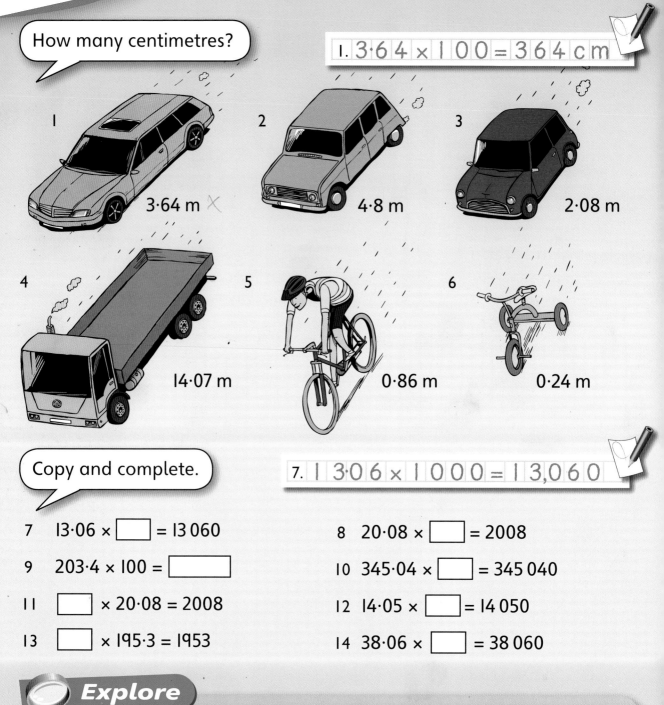

1. 3·64 m

2. 4·8 m

3. 2·08 m

4. 14·07 m

5. 0·86 m

6. 0·24 m

Copy and complete.

7. 13·06 × 1000 = 13,060

7 13·06 × ☐ = 13 060

8 20·08 × ☐ = 2008

9 203·4 × 100 = ☐

10 345·04 × ☐ = 345 040

11 ☐ × 20·08 = 2008

12 14·05 × ☐ = 14 050

13 ☐ × 195·3 = 1953

14 38·06 × ☐ = 38 060

Explore

How many amounts between £1 and £2 will multiply by 10 to give an exact number of pounds?

How many amounts between £1 and £10 will do the same?

6

Dividing by 10 and 100

1. Divide each planet number by 10. Find the star number that matches your answer.

1. a and k

a) 470

b) 550

c) 6060

d) 320

e) 7200

f) 5080

g) 4·7

h) 60·6

i) 508

j) 720

k) 47

l) 55

m) 3·2

n) 606

o) 5·5

p) 50·8

q) 32

r) 72

A cake weighs 2 kg. How many 10 g slices can be made? What other equal weight slices (multiples of 10 g) could you have?

Write the length of each pipeline in metres.

$$2. \ 3500 \div 100 = 35\,m$$

2
3500 cm

3
400 cm

4
5100 cm

5
6200 cm

6
21 000 cm

7
6700 cm

8
48 000 cm

9
900 cm

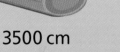
10
7600 cm

11
59 000 cm

12
800 cm

13
3900 cm

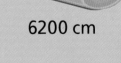
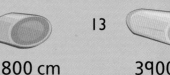

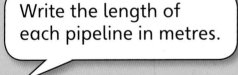

Which is the correct answer?
Write (a), (b), (c) or (d).

1 11 010 ÷ 10 is:
   a) 11 011   b) 1100
   c) 1101   d) 1011

2 12 000 ÷ 100 is:
   a) 120   b) 102
   c) 1200   d) 1020

3 3600 ÷ 10 is:
   a) 306   b) 36 000
   c) 36   d) 360

4 130 300 ÷ 100 is:
   a) 130 030   b) 13 030
   c) 130 303   d) 1303

5 480 300 ÷ 10 is:
   a) 48 030   b) 4 803 000
   c) 480   d) 4803

6 190 100 ÷ 10 is:
   a) 1900   b) 1901
   c) 1911   d) 19 010

7 200 100 ÷ 100 is:
   a) 201   b) 2000
   c) 2001   d) 2010

8 9800 ÷ 10 is:
   a) 98   b) 980
   c) 9808   d) 989

True or false?

9 2100 ÷ 100, then × 10, then ÷ 100 is 21.

10 One hundred and sixty thousand divided by one
    hundred is the same as sixteen thousand divided by ten.

11 Nine thousand and nine subtract nine, then divided
    by one hundred and then by ten equals nine.

How many times must one hundred
million be divided by 10 to get to 1?

How many litres?

12. 16 litres

12 16 000 ml   13 15 000 ml   14 31 000 ml   15 114 000 ml
16 1000 ml   17 45 000 ml   18 2000 ml   19 105 000 ml

Dividing by 10, 100 and 1000

Write the amount in pounds.

1. $507 \div 100 = £5.07$

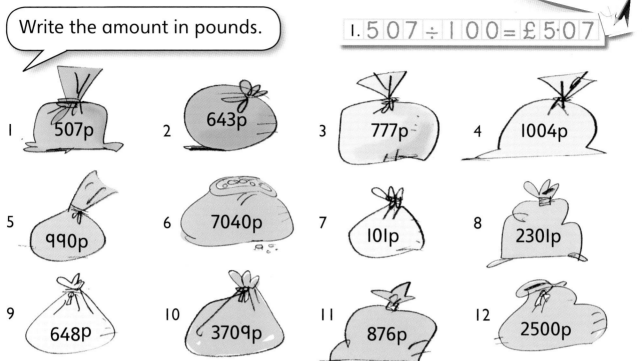

1. 507p
2. 643p
3. 777p
4. 1004p
5. 990p
6. 7040p
7. 101p
8. 2301p
9. 648P
10. 3709p
11. 876p
12. 2500p

Explore

How many amounts between $100 and $1000 can be given out in $10 and $100 notes so that there are equal numbers of each type of note? No more than nine $10 notes may be used.

Use division to complete these questions.

13. $1400m \div 1000 = 1.4km$

13 $1400\,m = \boxed{}\,km$

14 $4780\,m = \boxed{}\,km$

15 $3660\,ml = \boxed{}\,l$

16 $700\,ml = \boxed{}\,l$

17 $4880\,g = \boxed{}\,kg$

18 $5700\,m = \boxed{}\,km$

19 $6990\,ml = \boxed{}\,l$

20 $4820\,g = \boxed{}\,kg$

21 $3650\,m = \boxed{}\,km$

Find some amounts that, when divided by 10 or 100, leave you with three different coins? What about four coins?

9

How many 100 g weights are required to weigh each object? How many extra 10 g weights are needed?

1. 4260 ÷ 100 = 42·6
   42   100 g weights
    6   10 g weights

1
4260 g

2
33 790 g

3
5470 g

4
2180 g

5
6190 g

6
48 210 g

7
3940 g

8
12 590 g

Write the missing numbers.

9. 3010 ÷ 1000 = 3·01

9   3010 ÷ 1000 = [ ]

10   41·36 ÷ 1000 = [ ]

11   38·94 ÷ [ ] = 3·894

12   [ ] ÷ 100 = 0·036

13   90·9 ÷ 1000 = [ ]

14   3·6 ÷ [ ] = 0·036

15   [ ] ÷ 10 = 0·02

16   63·4 ÷ [ ] = 6·34

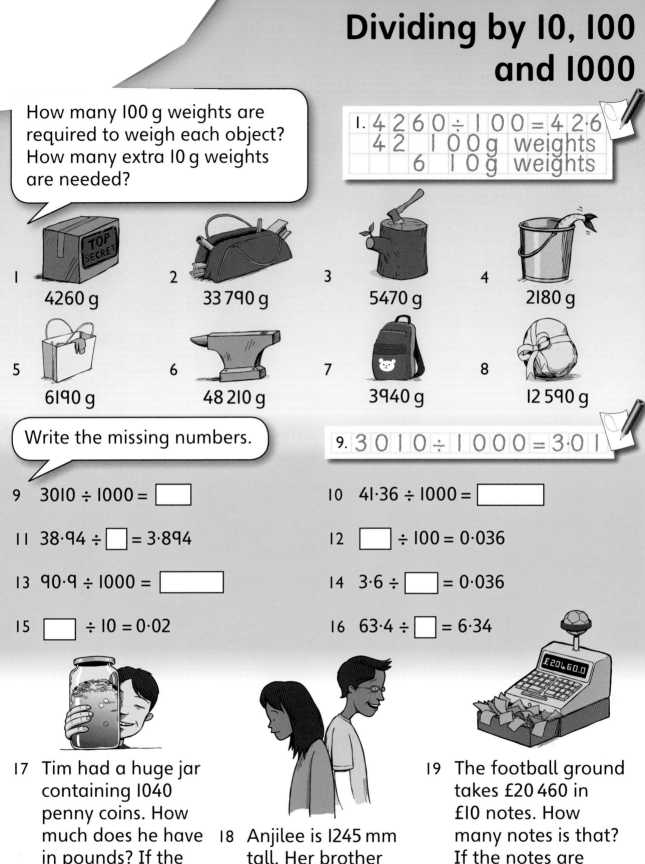

17   Tim had a huge jar containing 1040 penny coins. How much does he have in pounds? If the jar contained 1040 2p coins, how much would he have?

18   Anjilee is 1245 mm tall. Her brother Amit is 100 mm taller. How many metres tall is Amit?

19   The football ground takes £20 460 in £10 notes. How many notes is that? If the notes are bundled in groups of 10, how many bundles are there?

Multiplying and dividing

Write the position shown on each counting stick.

1. a) 18

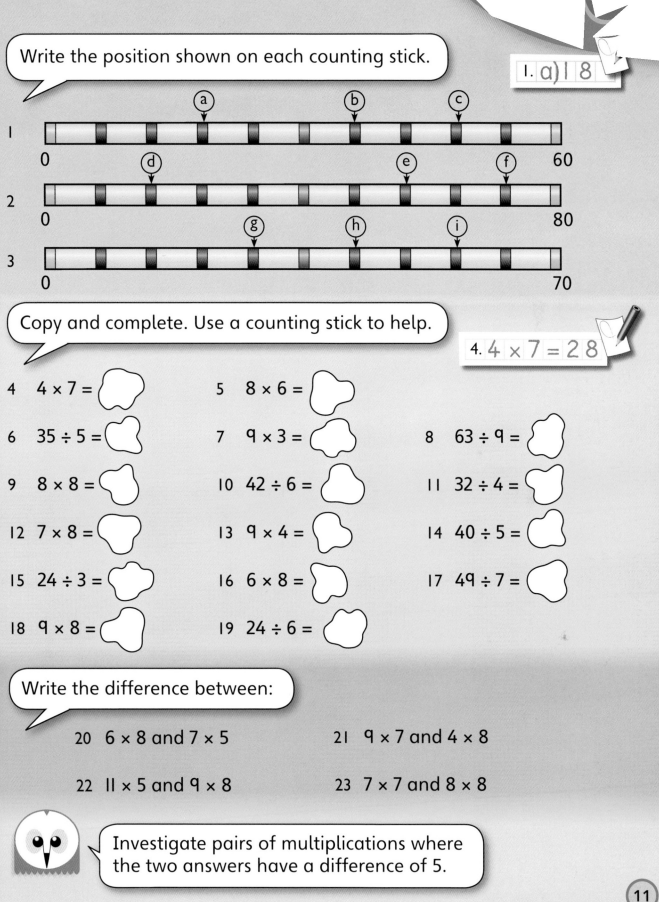

Copy and complete. Use a counting stick to help.

4. 4 × 7 = 28

4   4 × 7 =

5   8 × 6 =

6   35 ÷ 5 =

7   9 × 3 =

8   63 ÷ 9 =

9   8 × 8 =

10   42 ÷ 6 =

11   32 ÷ 4 =

12   7 × 8 =

13   9 × 4 =

14   40 ÷ 5 =

15   24 ÷ 3 =

16   6 × 8 =

17   49 ÷ 7 =

18   9 × 8 =

19   24 ÷ 6 =

Write the difference between:

20   6 × 8 and 7 × 5

21   9 × 7 and 4 × 8

22   11 × 5 and 9 × 8

23   7 × 7 and 8 × 8

Investigate pairs of multiplications where the two answers have a difference of 5.

11

Multiplying and dividing

Copy and complete these multiplication tables.

1

×	4	7	3	5
2				
8				
6				
9				

2

×	9	7	8	5
8				
4				
9				
6				

3

×	60	80	50	70
3				
2				
4				
6				

4

×	7	8	9	6
20				
40				
30				
50				

Explore

Use 0–9 digit cards and cards [×] [=]

Create different multiplications using 6 cards.

8 × 7 = 5 6   6 × 9 = 5 4

Here is a multiplication using more than 6 cards.

5 × 1 2 = 6 0

Can you make some more using more than 6 cards?

Copy and complete.

5   $24 \div 8 = \boxed{}$

6   $7 \times 7 = \boxed{}$

7   $8 \times 9 = \boxed{}$

8   $32 \div 4 = \boxed{}$

9   $42 \div 6 = \boxed{}$

10   $4 \times 8 = \boxed{}$

Multiplying and dividing

1. A chicken lays three eggs each day. How many weeks will it take to lay enough eggs to fill seven boxes, each containing six eggs.

2. The corner shop bought 500 kg of potatoes. It sells them in 6 kg bags. If it sells eight bags a day for a week, what weight of potatoes is left?

3. Jason saves £8 a week for 7 weeks, and then saves £7 a week for 9 weeks. How much has he saved?

4. Karen's book is 163 pages long. She reads nine pages a day for a week, then six pages a day for a week, then six pages a day for the next week. How many pages are left to read?

> Write the missing numbers.

5. $7 \times \boxed{} = 42$ 6. $\boxed{} \div 9 = 5$ 7. $36 \div \boxed{} = 6$ 8. $7 \times 8 = \boxed{}$

9. $72 \div \boxed{} = 8$ 10. $\boxed{} \times 9 = 45$ 11. $32 \div \boxed{} = 8$ 12. $21 \div \boxed{} = 7$

Explore

Table A

1	2	3	4	5	6	7	8
2	4	6	8	10	12	14	16
3	6	9	12	15			
						56	64

Table B

2						5	7
				3	6		
						2	1

Copy and complete Table A.

Copy and complete Table B to show the digital root of each number in the table.

To find the digital root, add the digits until you have a 1-digit number. Describe any patterns you notice.

15 ⟶ 6 (1 + 5)

56 ⟶ 11   2   (5 + 6 = 11, 1 + 1 = 2)

1 Here are three multiplication tables written in code. The tables are not in the correct order. Find the digit represented by each letter.

a × f = jc
b × f = he
g × f = f
h × f = ai
c × f = ge
f × f = ea
j × f = ca
d × f = bc
e × f = af

i × g = bf
f × g = de
a × g = ec
d × g = ei
c × g = g
h × g = fa
g × g = dh
e × g = cd
b × g = ab

s × q = lp
p × q = no
k × q = om
n × q = os
m × q = q
r × q = pk
q × q = nr
o × q = mn
l × q = kl

Choose a multiplication table to put into code. Challenge a friend to crack the code.

Find the missing numbers.

2 4 × ◯ = 320

3 500 ÷ ◯ = 20

4 600 ÷ ◯ = 12

5 ◯ × 60 = 180

6 320 ÷ ◯ = 80

7 ◯ × 7 = 280

8 70 × ◯ = 420

9 1080 ÷ ◯ = 120

10 770 ÷ ◯ = 70

Remainders

Complete these divisions. Write the remainder as a fraction.

1. $5\frac{1}{2}$

1	11 ÷ 2		2	33 ÷ 4

3   42 ÷ 5   4   23 ÷ 3

5   19 ÷ 6   6   31 ÷ 7

7   47 ÷ 10   8   29 ÷ 9

9   50 ÷ 8   10 27 ÷ 4

11 45 ÷ 6   12 85 ÷ 9

1	2	3	4	5	6	7	8	9	10
2	4	6	8	10	12	14	16	18	20
3	6	9	12	15	18	21	24	27	30
4	8	12	16	20	24	28	32	36	40
5	10	15	20	25	30	35	40	45	50
6	12	18	24	30	36	42	48	54	60
7	14	21	28	35	42	49	56	63	70
8	16	24	32	40	48	56	64	72	80
9	18	27	36	45	54	63	72	81	90
10	20	30	40	50	60	70	80	90	100

Investigate divisions that have remainders of $\frac{2}{3}$, $\frac{3}{4}$, $\frac{4}{5}$, $\frac{5}{6}$, $\frac{6}{7}$, . . .

Krishnan's mum has made 43 flapjacks. How many would each person get if they were shared equally between:

13. $43 ÷ 2 = 21\frac{1}{2}$

13   2 people   14   3 people

15   4 people   16   5 people

17   6 people   18   7 people

19   8 people   20   9 people

21   10 people?

Repeat for Jed's brother, who has made 67 macaroons.

Remainders

Write how many teams can be made.
Write the remainder as a fraction.

1. $14\frac{1}{3}$ teams

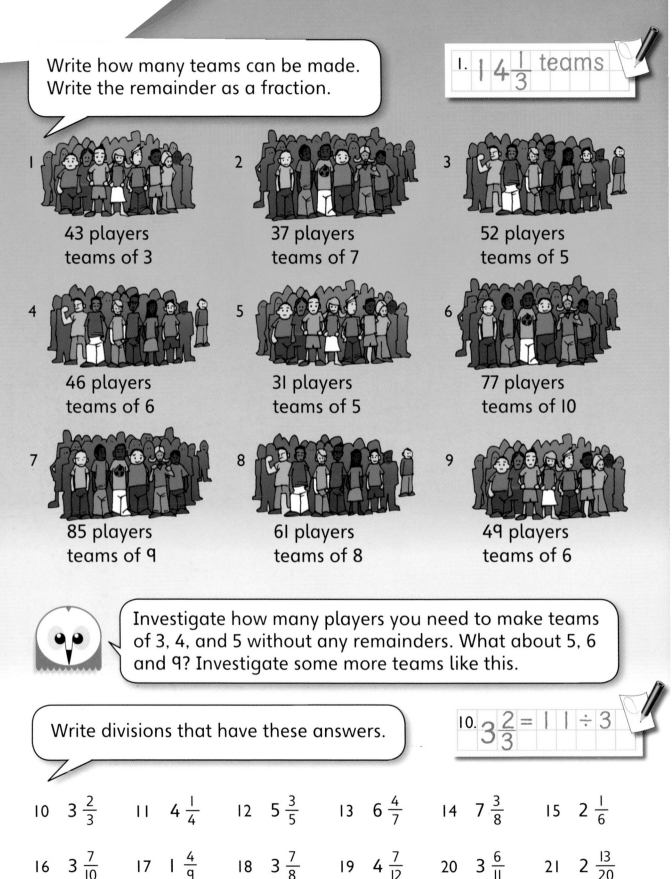

1
43 players
teams of 3

2
37 players
teams of 7

3
52 players
teams of 5

4
46 players
teams of 6

5
31 players
teams of 5

6
77 players
teams of 10

7
85 players
teams of 9

8
61 players
teams of 8

9
49 players
teams of 6

Investigate how many players you need to make teams of 3, 4, and 5 without any remainders. What about 5, 6 and 9? Investigate some more teams like this.

Write divisions that have these answers.

10. $3\frac{2}{3} = 11 \div 3$

10   $3\frac{2}{3}$ 11 $4\frac{1}{4}$ 12 $5\frac{3}{5}$ 13 $6\frac{4}{7}$ 14 $7\frac{3}{8}$ 15 $2\frac{1}{6}$

16   $3\frac{7}{10}$ 17 $1\frac{4}{9}$ 18 $3\frac{7}{8}$ 19 $4\frac{7}{12}$ 20 $3\frac{6}{11}$ 21 $2\frac{13}{20}$

Remainders

Tins of dog food are sold in boxes of 10. Write how many boxes as a decimal.

1. $32 \div 10 = 3.2$

1 32 tins

2 43 tins

3 19 tins

4 27 tins

5 58 tins

6 64 tins

7 130 tins

8 202 tins

Dog biscuits are sold in bags of 100. Write how many bags, as a decimal.

9. $136 \div 100 = 1.36$

9 136 biscuits

10 214 biscuits

11 326 biscuits

12 178 biscuits

13 291 biscuits

14 432 biscuits

15 906 biscuits

16 1008 biscuits

In March Rex the dog eats 13 biscuits a day. Estimate with your partner how many bags of biscuits he eats. Do the same for February.

Put these in order, smallest first, by writing each as a decimal.

17 A: $\dfrac{416}{100}$ B: $\dfrac{42}{10}$ C: $\dfrac{24}{5}$ D: $\dfrac{9}{2}$ E: $\dfrac{17}{4}$

18 A: $\dfrac{361}{100}$ B: $\dfrac{37}{10}$ C: $\dfrac{17}{5}$ D: $\dfrac{7}{2}$ E: $\dfrac{15}{4}$

19 A: $\dfrac{827}{100}$ B: $\dfrac{83}{10}$ C: $\dfrac{41}{5}$ D: $\dfrac{17}{2}$ E: $\dfrac{33}{4}$

1. $\dfrac{41}{10} = 4{\cdot}1$

1 $\dfrac{}{10} = 4{\cdot}1$

2 $ \div 2 = 2{\cdot}9$

3 $\dfrac{}{5} = 6{\cdot}6$

4 $ \div 10 = 3{\cdot}7$

5 $ \div 5 = 1{\cdot}7$

6 $\dfrac{}{4} = 3{\cdot}75$

7 $ \div 4 = 2{\cdot}25$

8 $\dfrac{}{10} = 6{\cdot}2$

9 $\dfrac{}{4} = 4{\cdot}5$

10 $ \div 2 = 19{\cdot}5$

11 $\dfrac{}{5} = 5{\cdot}4$

12 $ \div 5 = 7{\cdot}2$

> Write the two one-place decimals either side of the fraction.

13. $1{\cdot}3$ and $1{\cdot}4$

13 $\dfrac{4}{3}$

14 $\dfrac{13}{4}$

15 $\dfrac{27}{5}$

16 $\dfrac{83}{10}$

17 $\dfrac{41}{7}$

18 $\dfrac{16}{6}$

19 $\dfrac{11}{9}$

20 $\dfrac{13}{8}$

Explore

Use a calculator to explore different divisions that give answers between 6 and 7.

Start with divisions by 2, then by 3, then by 4, ….

$13 \div 2 = 6{\cdot}5$

For each divisor, write a division that gives an answer as close as possible to 6·5. How close can you get?

Odd and even

1

Use a multiplication square, or copy this one.

Colour or loop all the boxes that are the result of multiplying an odd number by an odd number.

Write what you notice about the coloured numbers.

Write what you notice about the remaining numbers in the table.

1	2	3	4	5	6	7	8	9	10
2	4	6	8	10	12	14	16	18	20
3	6	9	12	15	18	21	24	27	30
4	8	12	16	20	24	28	32	36	40
5	10	15	20	25	30	35	40	45	50
6	12	18	24	30	36	42	48	54	60
7	14	21	28	35	42	49	56	63	70
8	16	24	32	40	48	56	64	72	80
9	18	27	36	45	54	63	72	81	90
10	20	30	40	50	60	70	80	90	100

2 Copy and complete this table. Use 'O' for odd and 'E' for even.

×	O	E
O		
E		

Complete by writing odd or even.
Give an example to prove you are correct.

3. $3 \times odd = odd$
$3 \times 5 = 15$

3 $3 \times \boxed{} = odd$

4 $\boxed{} \times 4 = even$

5 $3 \times 2 \times \boxed{} = even$

6 $\boxed{} \times \boxed{} = odd$

7 $\boxed{} \times \boxed{} = even$

8 $\boxed{} \times 3 = even$

Odd and even

1. even

Write odd or even for each answer.

1 14 + 28 = ☐

2 35 + 41 = ☐

3 67 + 29 = ☐

4 78 − 24 = ☐

5 56 − 32 = ☐

6 148 + 169 = ☐

7 3004 − 192 = ☐

8 8176 − 385 = ☐

9 47 291 + 35 846 = ☐

Write odd or even for each missing word.

10. even

10 even + even = ☐

11 odd + odd = ☐

12 odd + ☐ = odd

13 even + ☐ = odd

14 even − ☐ = even

15 odd − ☐ = odd

16 odd − ☐ = even

17 ☐ − even = even

18 odd + odd + ☐ = odd

19 even + ☐ + even = even

20 odd + ☐ + even = even

21 ☐ + odd + even = odd

Explore

These are the pairs of factors of 18:   1 × 18   2 × 9   3 × 6
                                          O × E   E × O   O × E
All three are odd × even.

These are the pairs of factors of 20:   1 × 20   2 × 10   4 × 5
                                          O × E   E × E   E × O
Two are odd × even, one is even × even.

Investigate the oddness and evenness of pairs of factors for numbers up to 40. Are there any patterns?

I'm thinking of a number less than 10. If I double it, the answer is odd. What could my number be?

20

Odd and even

Write odd or even for each answer.

1. odd

1 $9 \times 7 =$ ☐

2 $8 \times 6 =$ ☐

3 $7 \times 12 =$ ☐

4 $35 \times 14 =$ ☐

5 $27 \times 16 =$ ☐

6 $38 \times 42 =$ ☐

7 $106 \times 25 =$ ☐

8 $74 \times 238 =$ ☐

9 $83 \times 419 =$ ☐

Write odd or even for each missing word.

10 even × even = ☐

11 odd × odd = ☐

12 even × odd = ☐

13 odd × even = ☐

14 ☐ × odd × odd = odd

15 even × even × ☐ = even

16 odd × even × odd = ☐

17 even × even × odd = ☐

18 odd × odd × odd × ☐ = even

True or false?

19 The product of two even numbers is always even.

20 The product of three even numbers can never be odd.

21 If the product of two numbers is even, then one of the numbers could be odd.

22 The product of two odd numbers is always odd.

23 The product of three odd numbers can never be even.

24 If the product of two numbers is odd, then one of the numbers could be even.

Five numbers are multiplied together:

☐ × ☐ × ☐ × ☐ × ☐ = even

What numbers could they be (e.g. odd × odd × ...)?

Cubic numbers

Explore

The number of cubes needed to make a cube of edge size 2 is:

2 × 2 × 2 = 8.

The number of cubes needed to make a cube of edge size 3 is:

3 × 3 × 3 = 27.

8 and 27 are cubic numbers.

Find some more cubic numbers.
You can use a calculator to help you.

Investigate which cubic numbers are odd and which are even.
Are there any patterns?

Explore

Make a list of the odd numbers:

1, 3, 5, 7, 9, 11, . . .

Create a triangle by writing one number in the first row, the next two in the second row, the next three in the third row, and so on:

1
3   5
7   9   11

Investigate the total of each row of numbers.
Describe any patterns you notice.

Common multiples

Use the multiplication square to help you write all the numbers in the square that are multiples of:

1   7   2   4   3   9

Find the numbers that are common multiples of:

1	2	3	4	5	6	7	8	9	10
2	4	6	8	10	12	14	16	18	20
3	6	9	12	15	18	21	24	27	30
4	8	12	16	20	24	28	32	36	40
5	10	15	20	25	30	35	40	45	50
6	12	18	24	30	36	42	48	54	60
7	14	21	28	35	42	49	56	63	70
8	16	24	32	40	48	56	64	72	80
9	18	27	36	45	54	63	72	81	90
10	20	30	40	50	60	70	80	90	100

4   2 and 3   5   3 and 4

6   2 and 7   7   4 and 6

8   4 and 8   9   4 and 5

Explore

12 is a common multiple of 2, 3 and 4. Find another number that is a common multiple of consecutive numbers.

Find the smallest common multiples of:

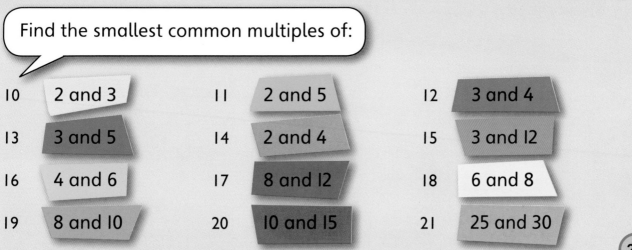

10   2 and 3   11   2 and 5   12   3 and 4

13   3 and 5   14   2 and 4   15   3 and 12

16   4 and 6   17   8 and 12   18   6 and 8

19   8 and 10   20   10 and 15   21   25 and 30

Common multiples

Balls: 21, 42, 8, 32, 60, 50, 14
40, 16, 24, 20, 48, 18, 23, 36

Write which of the ball numbers are multiples of:

1	4	2	3	3	2 and 3	4	3 and 4
5	4 and 5	6	2 and 7	7	3 and 7	8	5 and 8
9	2, 3 and 4	10	3, 4 and 5				

Write one more ball number that belongs to each set.

Write five ball numbers that are not multiples of 2, 3, 4 or 10.

Copy each grid. Write in each box the number that is the smallest common multiple of both the row and the column.

11

	2	3	4
5			
6			
7			

12

	2	8	5
3			
9			
4			

13

	10	4	6
5			
20			
2			

14

	15	10	2
3			
9			
4			

Common multiples

For each set of numbers, write three common multiples.

1	2 7	2	3 4	3	5 3
4	6 10	5	4 5	6	5 15
7	25 20	8	4 9	9	5 8
10	2 6 5	11	3 4 5	12	10 15 25

Write the smallest common multiple of each set.

Explore

Use one set of 2–9 cards.

Investigate all the different possible pairs of cards and the smallest common multiple of each pair. You can record them in a table:

×	2	3	4
2	2	6	4
3			
4			

How many different common multiples are there?

Common multiples

1   I am a common multiple of 3 and 7. The difference between my two digits is 4.

2   I am the smallest common multiple of the third square number and the number of lines of symmetry of a regular hexagon.

3   I am a common multiple of 4 and 6. My two digits have a total of 12.

4   I am a common multiple of 2, 5 and 3. I have three digits that have a total of 9.

5   I am the smallest common multiple of the number of sides of an octagon and the number of edges of a cube.

6   I am a common multiple of 3, 4, and 6 and I am also a square number.

Explore

For each of the pairs of fractions below, look at the denominators.

Write the smallest common multiple.

Use this as a denominator to change them into equivalent fractions.

Add the fractions together.

$\frac{1}{2}$ $\frac{2}{3}$

6

$\frac{3}{6}$ $\frac{4}{6}$

$\frac{3}{6} + \frac{4}{6} = \frac{7}{6}$

a) $\frac{1}{2}$ $\frac{2}{3}$

b) $\frac{4}{5}$ $\frac{3}{4}$

c) $\frac{2}{3}$ $\frac{3}{4}$

d) $\frac{7}{10}$ $\frac{3}{5}$

e) $\frac{5}{6}$ $\frac{1}{8}$

f) $\frac{1}{3}$ $\frac{5}{9}$

g) $\frac{1}{2}$ $\frac{2}{3}$ $\frac{1}{4}$

h) $\frac{1}{2}$ $\frac{3}{5}$ $\frac{7}{10}$

i) $\frac{3}{4}$ $\frac{7}{8}$ $\frac{5}{12}$

Two fractions have a total of $\frac{7}{12}$. They have different denominators. What fractions could they be?

Parallelograms

Copy these parallelograms onto squared paper.

1

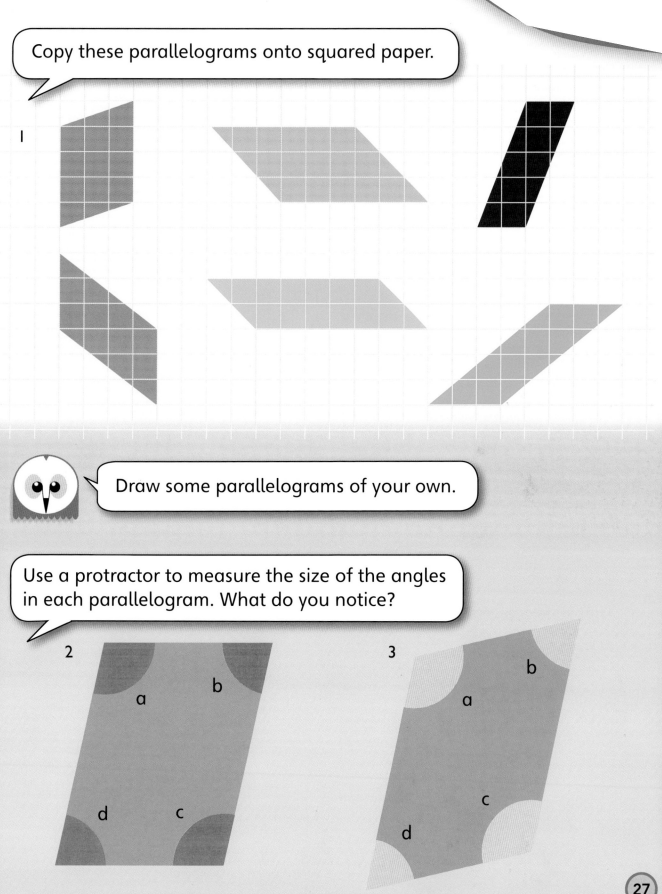

Draw some parallelograms of your own.

Use a protractor to measure the size of the angles in each parallelogram. What do you notice?

2

a b

d c

3

b

a

c

d

Quadrilaterals

Write the name of each quadrilateral.
Choose from the labels.

1. parallelogram

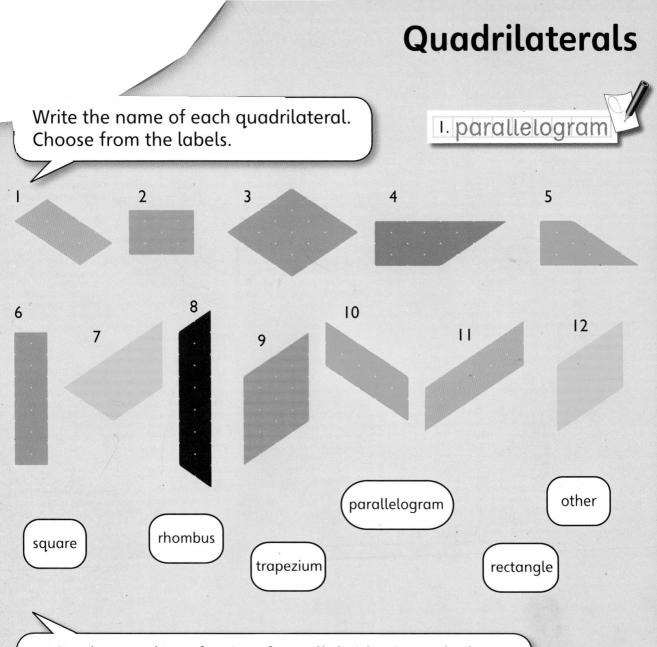

square

rhombus

trapezium

parallelogram

rectangle

other

Write the number of pairs of parallel sides in each shape.
Write which shapes have perpendicular sides.

Explore

Draw any triangle on a sheet of paper, and then cut it out.

Use it to trace an identical triangle and cut this out.

Arrange the two triangles to make parallelograms.

Repeat for different shaped triangles.

Quadrilaterals

Explore

Use dotted paper to make a parallelogram within a 4 × 4 square. Here are two. How many can you make altogether?

True or false?

1   A rhombus is a parallelogram with four equal sides.

2   A trapezium has one pair of parallel sides.

3   A square is a type of rhombus.

4   A rectangle is a type of parallelogram.

5   A parallelogram has two pairs of equal sides.

6   A parallelogram always has line symmetry.

7   A trapezium can have a right angle.

8   A parallelogram can have two obtuse angles.

9   The angles of a rhombus are never equal.

10   A trapezium is always symmetrical.

11   The diagonals of a parallelogram can be the same length.

12   If one angle of a rhombus is 90°, it must be a square.

Explore

Draw this rhombus on isometric paper.

Draw some others.

Draw the diagonals of each rhombus.

What do you notice about where the diagonals cross?

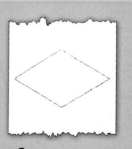

Quadrilaterals

Use dotted paper to make a trapezium within a 3 × 4 rectangle.

Here are four trapeziums. How many more can you make? How many altogether?

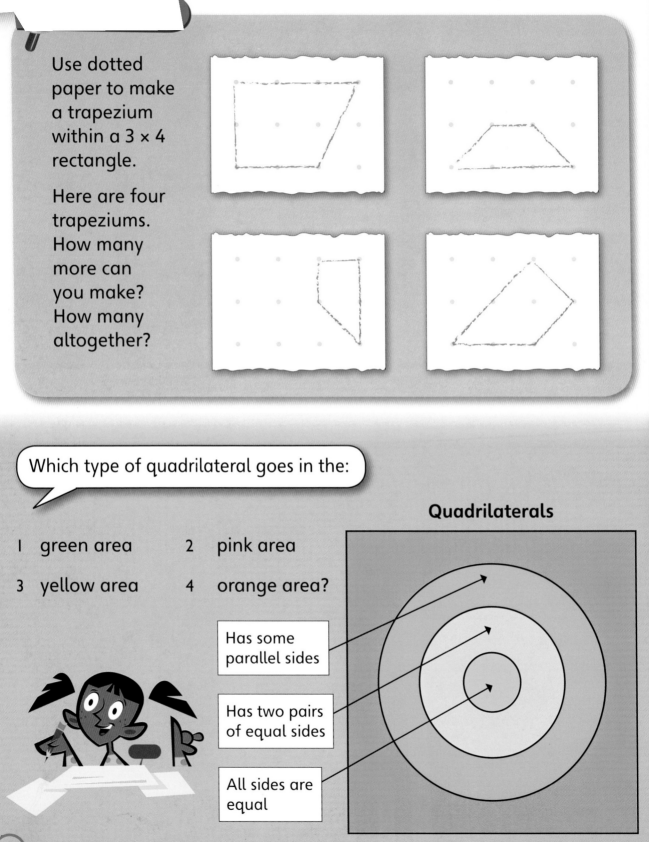

Which type of quadrilateral goes in the:

1 green area

2 pink area

3 yellow area

4 orange area?

Has some parallel sides

Has two pairs of equal sides

All sides are equal

Quadrilaterals

Kites and arrowheads

Copy these kites and arrowheads onto squared paper.

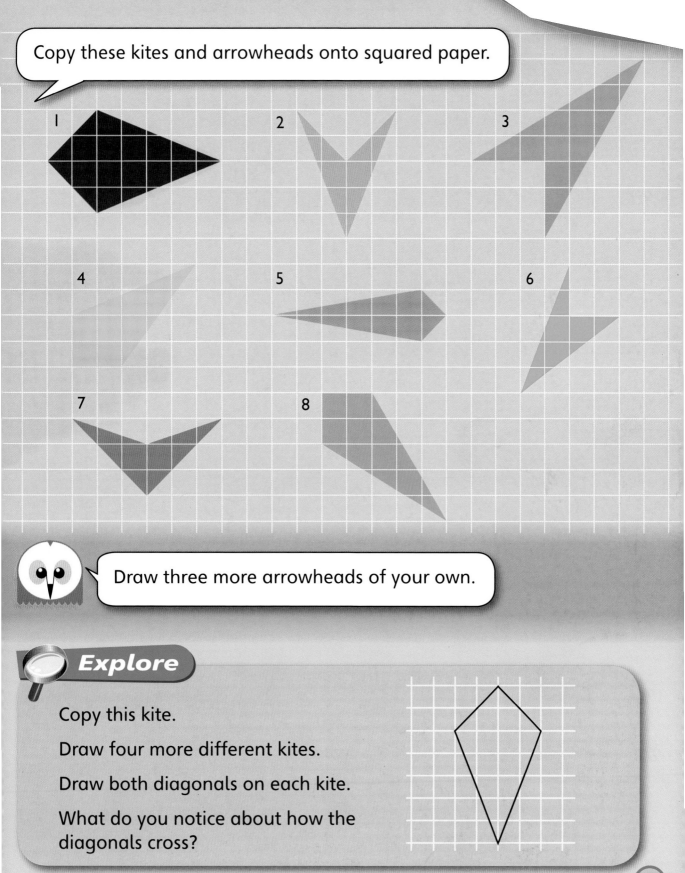

Draw three more arrowheads of your own.

Explore

Copy this kite.

Draw four more different kites.

Draw both diagonals on each kite.

What do you notice about how the diagonals cross?

Quadrilaterals

Write the name of each shape. Choose from the labels.

1. arrowhead

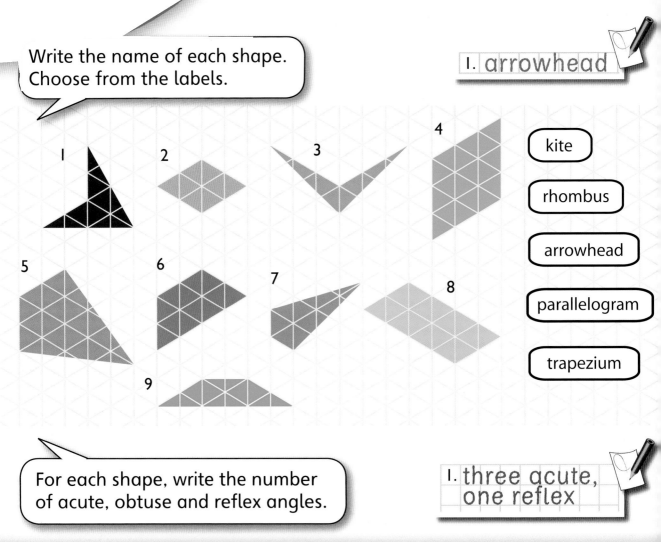

kite

rhombus

arrowhead

parallelogram

trapezium

For each shape, write the number of acute, obtuse and reflex angles.

1. three acute, one reflex

True or false?

10 A kite has two pairs of equal sides.

11 An arrowhead can have a right angle.

12 An arrowhead has two pairs of equal sides.

13 An arrowhead has a reflex angle.

14 A kite need not be symmetrical.

15 A kite always has one pair of parallel sides.

16 A kite always has two pairs of equal angles.

17 If you draw a kite and make all sides equal, it is a rhombus.

18 An arrowhead has line symmetry.

Write a true or false question for your partner to answer.

Quadrilaterals

Copy and complete the table. For each statement and shape colour the box the correct colour.

1

	square	rectangle	parallelogram	rhombus	trapezium	kite	arrowhead
Has 4 sides							
Has all sides the same length							
Has one pair of opposite sides parallel							
Has two pairs of opposite sides parallel							
Has opposite sides equal							
Has adjacent sides equal							
Has line symmetry							
Has a right angle							
Has an obtuse angle							
Has a reflex angle							

■ always true   □ sometimes true   ▨ never true

Explore

Here are two quadrilaterals drawn on 3 × 3 dotted paper.

It is possible to draw 16 different quadrilaterals altogether. Can you find them all?

These, for example, are not different.

How many of the 16 are (a) parallelograms, (b) trapeziums, (c) kites, (d) arrowheads?

33

Pictograms

A pictogram to show the length of songs on the radio, in minutes and seconds

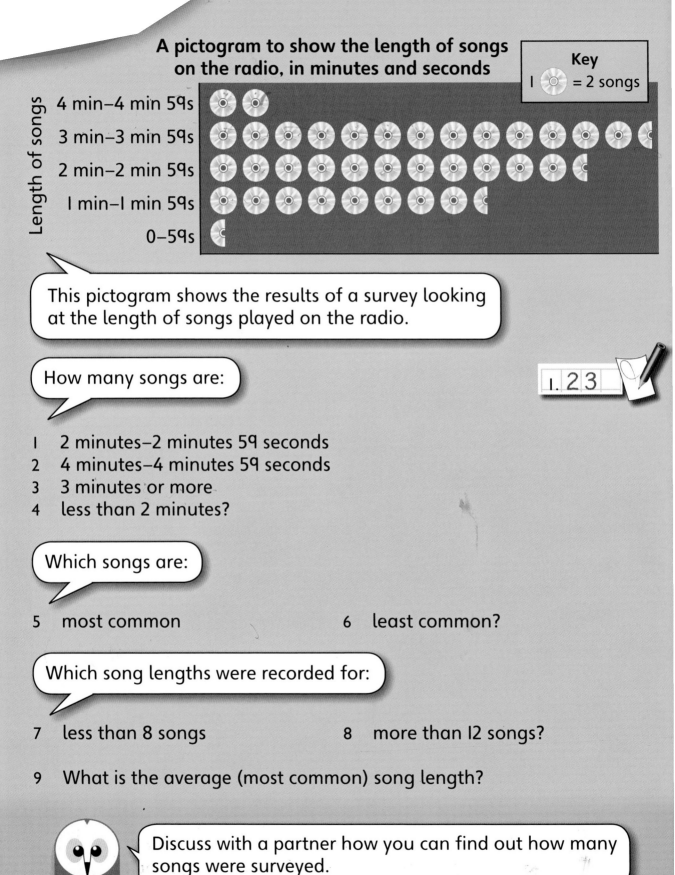

Key
1 ⊙ = 2 songs

Length of songs:
- 4 min–4 min 59s
- 3 min–3 min 59s
- 2 min–2 min 59s
- 1 min–1 min 59s
- 0–59s

This pictogram shows the results of a survey looking at the length of songs played on the radio.

How many songs are:

1.23

1   2 minutes–2 minutes 59 seconds
2   4 minutes–4 minutes 59 seconds
3   3 minutes or more
4   less than 2 minutes?

Which songs are:

5   most common

6   least common?

Which song lengths were recorded for:

7   less than 8 songs

8   more than 12 songs?

9   What is the average (most common) song length?

Discuss with a partner how you can find out how many songs were surveyed.

Pictograms

A pictogram to show the length of children's programmes on television, in minutes

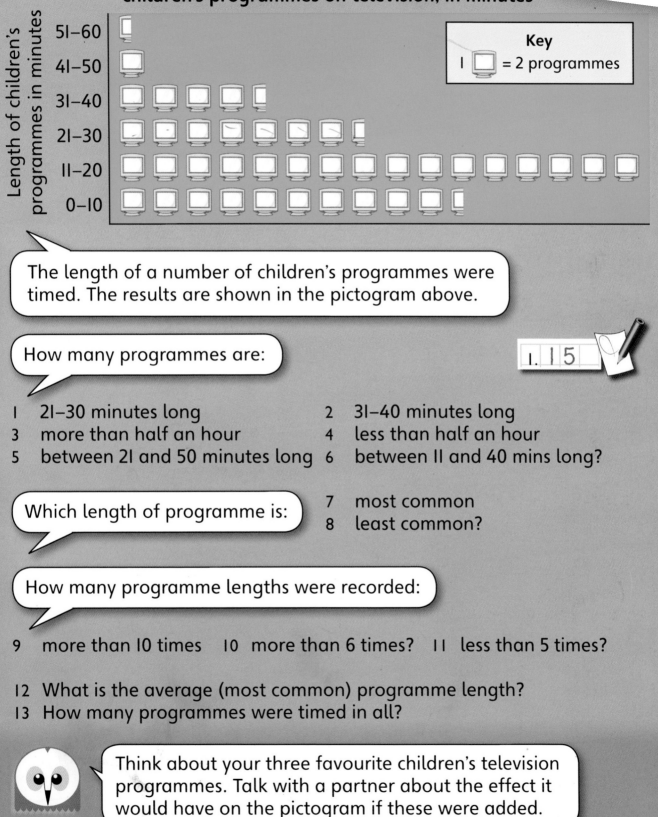

Length of children's programmes in minutes

51–60	🖥
41–50	🖥
31–40	🖥🖥🖥🖥🖥
21–30	🖥🖥🖥🖥🖥🖥🖥🖥
11–20	🖥🖥🖥🖥🖥🖥🖥🖥🖥🖥🖥🖥🖥🖥🖥🖥
0–10	🖥🖥🖥🖥🖥🖥🖥🖥🖥🖥

Key

I 🖥 = 2 programmes

The length of a number of children's programmes were timed. The results are shown in the pictogram above.

How many programmes are:

1. 15

1 21–30 minutes long
2 31–40 minutes long
3 more than half an hour
4 less than half an hour
5 between 21 and 50 minutes long
6 between 11 and 40 mins long?

Which length of programme is:

7 most common
8 least common?

How many programme lengths were recorded:

9 more than 10 times
10 more than 6 times?
11 less than 5 times?

12 What is the average (most common) programme length?
13 How many programmes were timed in all?

Think about your three favourite children's television programmes. Talk with a partner about the effect it would have on the pictogram if these were added.

Pictograms

Totals when adding pairs of cards

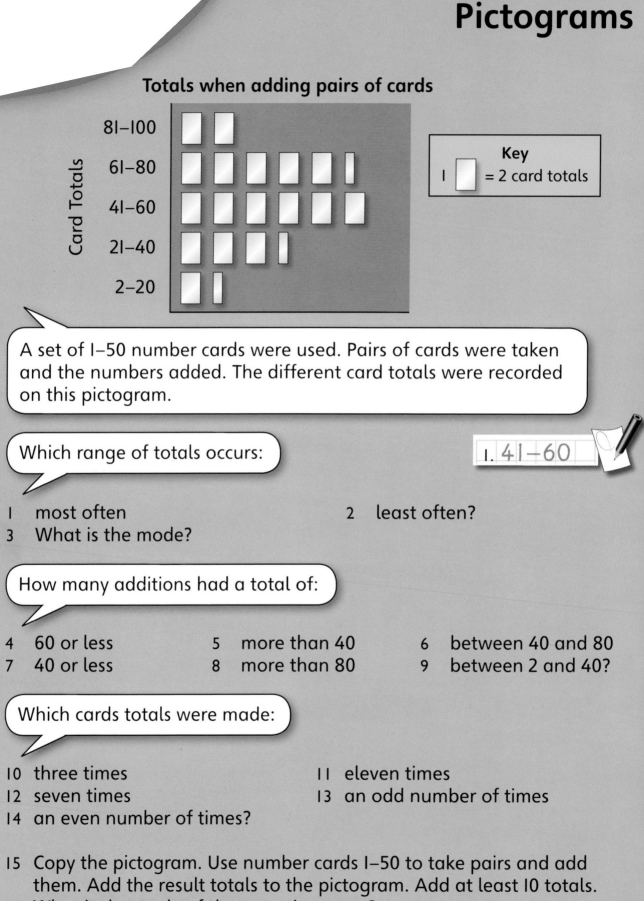

A set of 1–50 number cards were used. Pairs of cards were taken and the numbers added. The different card totals were recorded on this pictogram.

Which range of totals occurs:

1. 41–60

1   most often
2   least often?
3   What is the mode?

How many additions had a total of:

4   60 or less
5   more than 40
6   between 40 and 80
7   40 or less
8   more than 80
9   between 2 and 40?

Which cards totals were made:

10 three times
11 eleven times
12 seven times
13 an odd number of times
14 an even number of times?

15 Copy the pictogram. Use number cards 1–50 to take pairs and add them. Add the result totals to the pictogram. Add at least 10 totals.
16 What is the mode of the new pictogram?

Pictograms

Copy this tally chart.

1–15	16–30	31–45	46–60	61–75	76–90
‖	ЖТ ‖	ЖТ ЖТ ‖	ЖТ ЖТ		ЖТ ||||	||||

1 Work with a partner using 1–20 number cards. Take 4 and add them together. Add a tally mark to the appropriate column. Repeat this twelve times.

2 Draw a frequency table based on your tally chart.

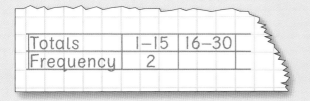

Totals	1–15	16–30
Frequency	2	

3 Draw a pictogram to represent your results. Remember to include a title. Use the key below:

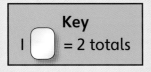

Key

| = 2 totals

4 What range of card totals is the mode?

How many additions made a total of:

5 1–15

6 more than 30

7 less than 46

8 between 31 and 60?

9 What range of totals was least common?

Some totals seem to be more common than others. Discuss with a partner why you think this is. Can you demonstrate it?

Look at the graph. Use it to answer the questions.

Graph to show the number of packets of crisps eaten each month

1 How is the information grouped?
2 How many packets of crisps eaten per month is the most common?
3 How many children ate 21–25 packets of crisps per month?
4 How many children ate 1–5 packets?
5 How many children took part in the survey?
6 For packets of crisps, what is the range?

How many children ate:

7 more than 20 packets?
8 fewer than 11 packets?
9 between 10 and 26 packets?

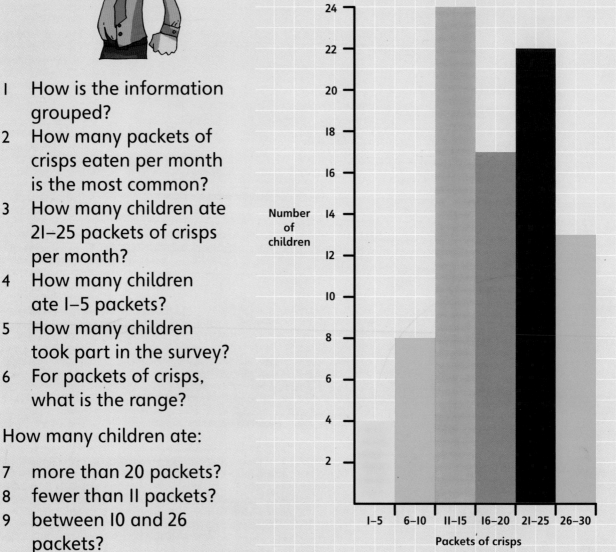

Discuss with a partner the number of packets of crisps you eat each month. Which bar(s) on the graph would change if you were to add to your data?

Grouping data

Minutes of TV watched each day

1. Look at the way the information is grouped. Is it sensible?

2. Draw a frequency table to represent the information.

3. Draw a bar chart like this using the frequency table.

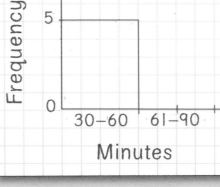

4. What is the time range for watching TV?

5. Which time period is the most common?

How many children watched for:

6. more than $2\frac{1}{2}$ hours

7. an hour and a half or less

8. between $1\frac{1}{2}$ and $2\frac{1}{2}$ hours

9. more than $\frac{1}{8}$ of a day?

Draw a frequency table to show the number of hours of TV watched each day by people in your class?

Grouping data

Look at the table. It gives information about how many hot drinks people drank on one day.

Cups	1	2	3	4	5	6	7	8	9	10	11	12
Tallies	I	II	Ж	Ж I	Ж	III	III	I	II	I	I	I

1   Group the data in the following way: 1–2 cups, 3–4 cups, 5–6 cups …

2   Draw a frequency table.   3   Draw and label a bar graph.

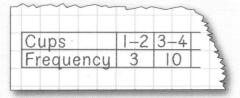

Cups	1–2	3–4
Frequency	3	10

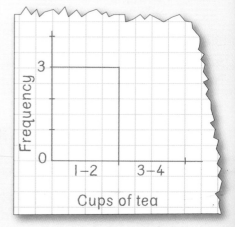

4   How many cups were drunk most frequently?

5   How many cups were drunk least frequently?

6   How many people drank:

   a)   more than six cups?

   b)   fewer than three cups?

   c)   more than two and fewer than nine cups?

7   True or false: half the people asked drank up to six cups per day?

8   If each day was the same, how many cups would each group drink in one week?

If you added the adults in your house to this information, would it affect the most common frequency?

Metres, centimetres and millimetres

Write the length of each dog in centimetres and millimetres.

1. 0·36 m = 36 cm
   36 cm = 360 mm

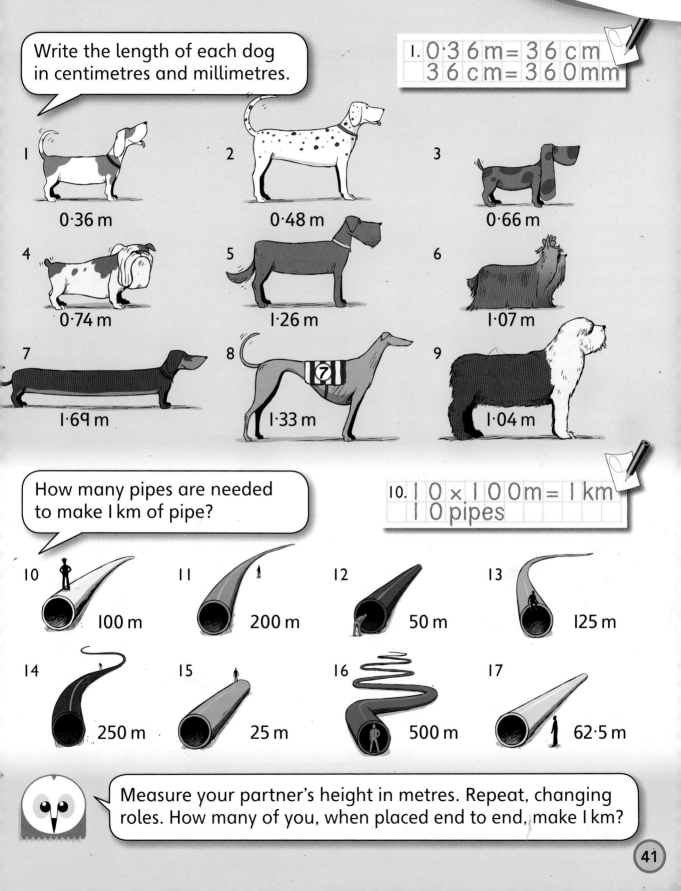

1. 0·36 m

2. 0·48 m

3. 0·66 m

4. 0·74 m

5. 1·26 m

6. 1·07 m

7. 1·69 m

8. 1·33 m

9. 1·04 m

How many pipes are needed to make 1 km of pipe?

10. 10 × 100 m = 1 km
    10 pipes

10. 100 m

11. 200 m

12. 50 m

13. 125 m

14. 250 m

15. 25 m

16. 500 m

17. 62·5 m

Measure your partner's height in metres. Repeat, changing roles. How many of you, when placed end to end, make 1 km?

41

Write the length and width of each paper in metres and in millimetres.

1. 0·38m × 0·334m
380mm × 334mm

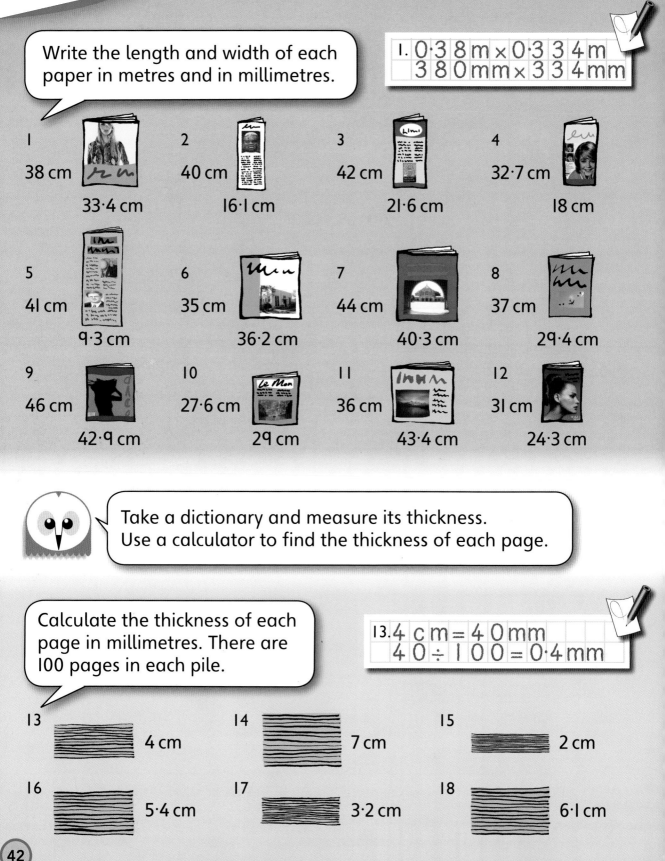

1
38 cm
33·4 cm

2
40 cm
16·1 cm

3
42 cm
21·6 cm

4
32·7 cm
18 cm

5
41 cm
9·3 cm

6
35 cm
36·2 cm

7
44 cm
40·3 cm

8
37 cm
29·4 cm

9
46 cm
42·9 cm

10
27·6 cm
29 cm

11
36 cm
43·4 cm

12
31 cm
24·3 cm

Take a dictionary and measure its thickness.
Use a calculator to find the thickness of each page.

Calculate the thickness of each page in millimetres. There are 100 pages in each pile.

13. 4 cm = 40 mm
40 ÷ 100 = 0·4 mm

13
4 cm

14
7 cm

15
2 cm

16
5·4 cm

17
3·2 cm

18
6·1 cm

Kilometres, metres, centimetres and millimetres

How many children are needed to run a relay race of at least 1 km when each child runs:

1. 4 children

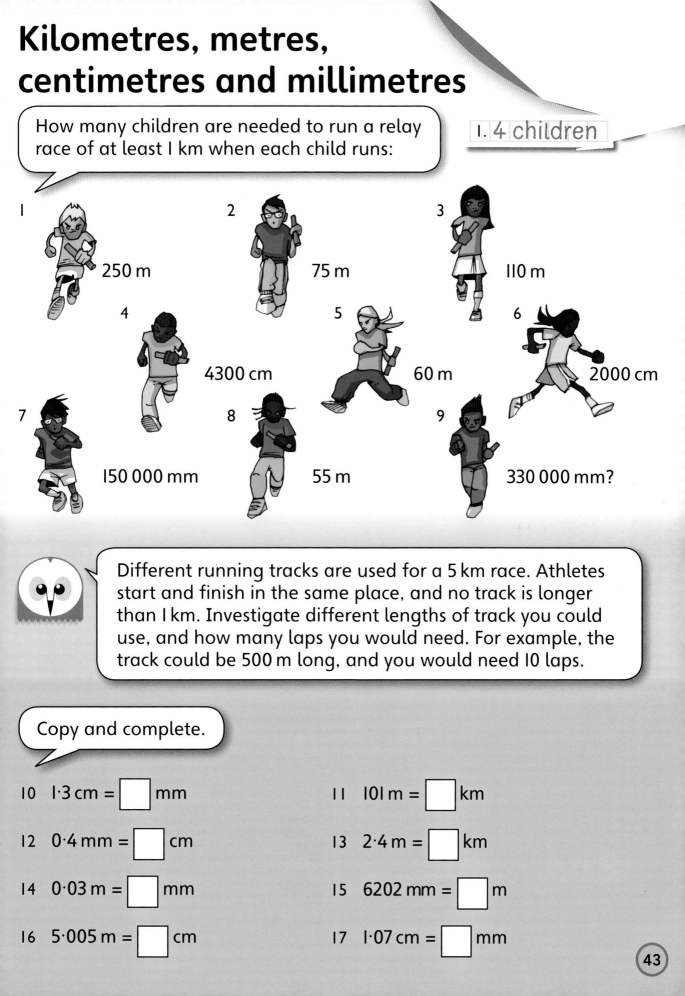

1   250 m

2   75 m

3   110 m

4   4300 cm

5   60 m

6   2000 cm

7   150 000 mm

8   55 m

9   330 000 mm?

Different running tracks are used for a 5 km race. Athletes start and finish in the same place, and no track is longer than 1 km. Investigate different lengths of track you could use, and how many laps you would need. For example, the track could be 500 m long, and you would need 10 laps.

Copy and complete.

10   1·3 cm = ☐ mm

11   101 m = ☐ km

12   0·4 mm = ☐ cm

13   2·4 m = ☐ km

14   0·03 m = ☐ mm

15   6202 mm = ☐ m

16   5·005 m = ☐ cm

17   1·07 cm = ☐ mm

Metres and miles

Write each distance in kilometres and in miles.

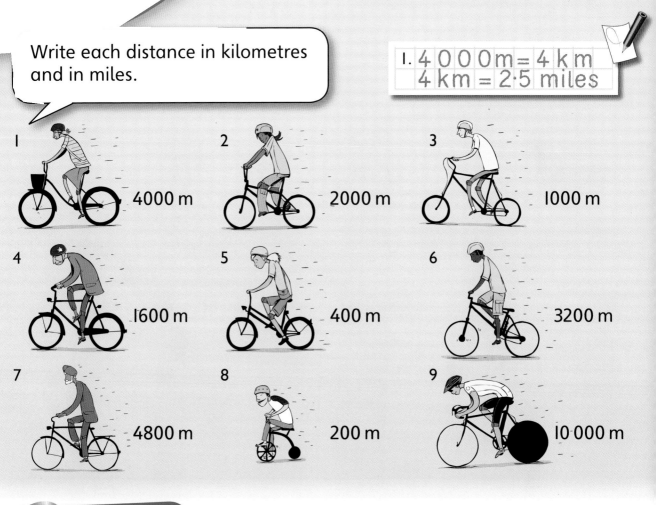

1   4000 m

2   2000 m

3   1000 m

4   1600 m

5   400 m

6   3200 m

7   4800 m

8   200 m

9   10·000 m

Explore

How many metres long is your classroom? Investigate what this length is in inches. How about in feet? In yards?

10   Simon has a ream of paper (500 sheets). It is 8·5 cm thick. He wants to stack 10 reams. How many metres tall will it be? How thick is each piece of paper?

11   A rabbit grows 4 cm each month for the first 10 months. If it starts at 64 mm, what is its length in metres after 10 months?

12   A packet of 100 pens is 82 cm long. How wide is each pen? How many pens will fit in a box 0·4 m long?

Kilograms and grams

Write the weight of each cake in kilograms.

1. $942\,g = 0.942\,kg$

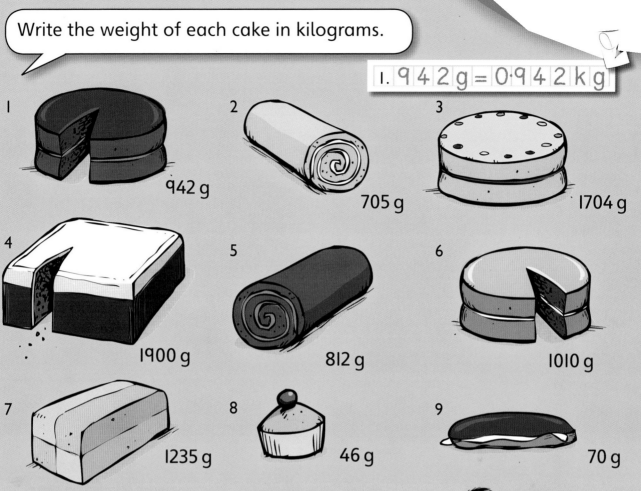

1. 942 g

2. 705 g

3. 1704 g

4. 1900 g

5. 812 g

6. 1010 g

7. 1235 g

8. 46 g

9. 70 g

10. Sarah weighed 3·5 kg when she was born. She gained 125 g each week. How heavy was she in kilograms after 4 weeks? After 8 weeks?

11. Craig's bag of tools weighs 9·4 kg. If he takes out two sledgehammers weighing 3400 g each, how heavy is his bag now?

12. Tara is going backpacking. Her rucksack weighs 26 050 g. The maximum amount it can weigh is 25 kg. How much weight must she lose?

Estimate how much a cat weighs. About how many cats weigh the same as a person? Estimate how much an elephant weighs. About how many people weigh the same as an elephant?

Tonnes, kilograms and grams

Write the weight of each book in grams.

1. `2030g`

1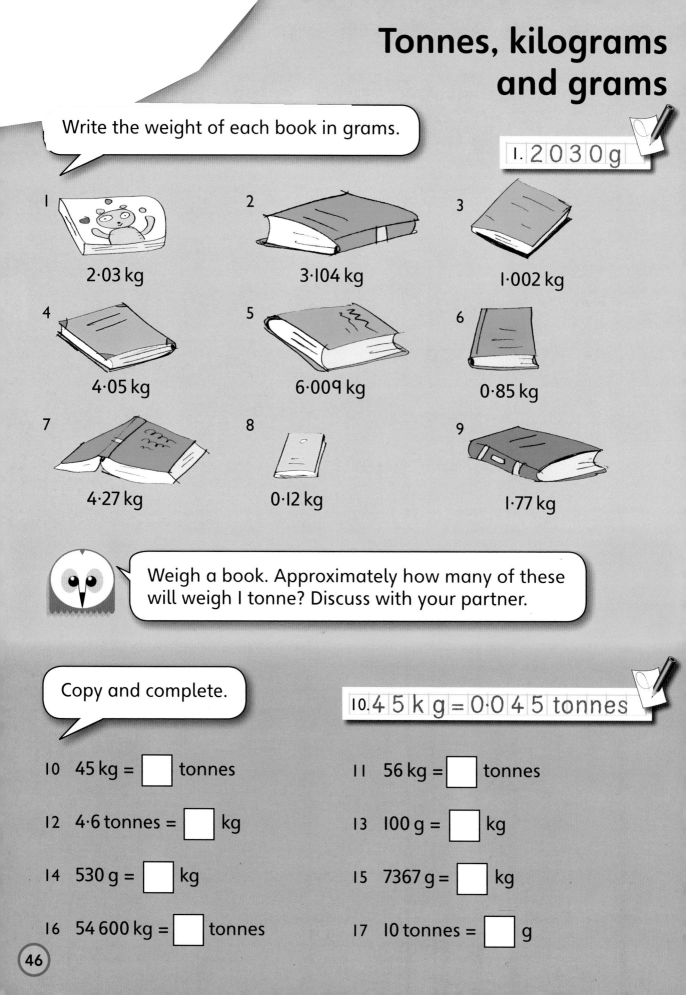
2·03 kg

2
3·104 kg

3
1·002 kg

4
4·05 kg

5
6·009 kg

6
0·85 kg

7
4·27 kg

8
0·12 kg

9
1·77 kg

Weigh a book. Approximately how many of these will weigh 1 tonne? Discuss with your partner.

Copy and complete.

10. `45 kg = 0·045 tonnes`

10   45 kg = ☐ tonnes

11   56 kg = ☐ tonnes

12   4·6 tonnes = ☐ kg

13   100 g = ☐ kg

14   530 g = ☐ kg

15   7367 g = ☐ kg

16   54 600 kg = ☐ tonnes

17   10 tonnes = ☐ g

Kilograms, grams, pounds and ounces

Write each weight in kilograms.

1. 2·2 lb = 1 kg

1 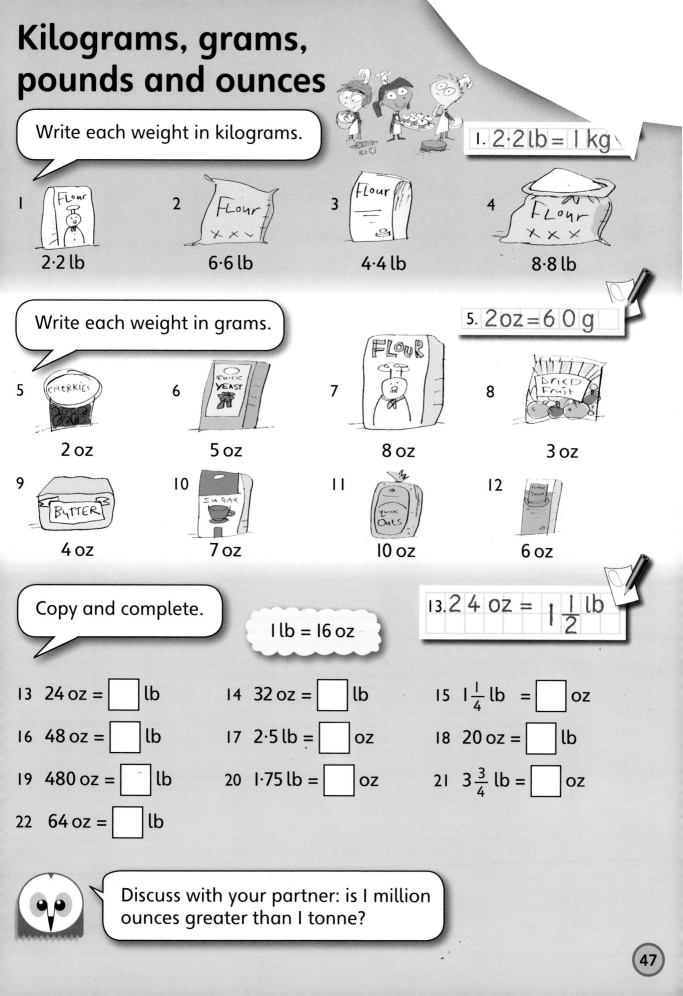 2·2 lb

2 6·6 lb

3 4·4 lb

4 8·8 lb

Write each weight in grams.

5. 2 oz = 60 g

5 CHERRIES 2 oz

6 QUICK YEAST 5 oz

7 FLOUR 8 oz

8 Dried Fruit 3 oz

9 BUTTER 4 oz

10 SUGAR 7 oz

11 Quick Oats 10 oz

12 ICING SUGAR 6 oz

Copy and complete.

1 lb = 16 oz

13. 24 oz = $1\frac{1}{2}$ lb

13 24 oz = ☐ lb

14 32 oz = ☐ lb

15 $1\frac{1}{4}$ lb = ☐ oz

16 48 oz = ☐ lb

17 2·5 lb = ☐ oz

18 20 oz = ☐ lb

19 480 oz = ☐ lb

20 1·75 lb = ☐ oz

21 $3\frac{3}{4}$ lb = ☐ oz

22 64 oz = ☐ lb

Discuss with your partner: is 1 million ounces greater than 1 tonne?

47

Problems

1 A 2 lb jar of honey is heavier than a 1 kg bag of sugar.

2 Five pounds is approximately the same as two and a quarter kilograms.

3 Ten 10 kg bags of coal are equal to one tenth of a tonne of coal.

4 220 lb is twice as much as 50 kg.

5 A cake recipe uses 4 oz butter and twice that amount of sugar. The sugar is about $\frac{1}{4}$ kg.

6 One pound is equal to 480 g.

7 One tonne is identical to 1 000 000 grams.

Explore

Find ways to work out these questions. Use a calculator to help!

How many 10 lb weights make up 1 tonne?

If 14 lb = 1 stone, how many stones are there in 1 tonne?

If 112 lb make a hundredweight, how many hundredweight are there in 1 tonne?

Angles

Estimate the size of each angle. Use your protractor to measure it.

1. estimate
   measure

With a partner, draw an angle close to 72°. Measure each other's angle. Who was closest? Now try it for 136°.

Use a protractor to draw these angles.

Acute angles: 7   60°   8   75°   9   38°

Obtuse angles: 10   110°   11   155°   12   127°

Calculate, in degrees, the angle for each turn (a) clockwise and (b) anticlockwise.

1. a) 1 3 5°
   b) 2 2 5°
   Total 3 6 0°

1	N to SE	2	SW to NW	3	S to SE
4	NE to SW	5	NW to SW	6	E to SW

For each of these clockwise turns, calculate the anticlockwise turn that will bring you to the same position.

7	120°	8	310°	9	155°	10	345°
11	265°	12	72°	13	183°	14	247°

Measure all the angles meeting at a point. Add them together.

15
a b
d c

16
a
b
d
c

Angles A, B and C meet at a point.

Angle A is $\frac{1}{2}$ the size of angle B and $\frac{1}{3}$ the size of angle C. What size are the angles?

Angles at a point

Calculate the angle of each slice of pizza.

1. 140 + 170 = 310°
   360 − 310 = 50

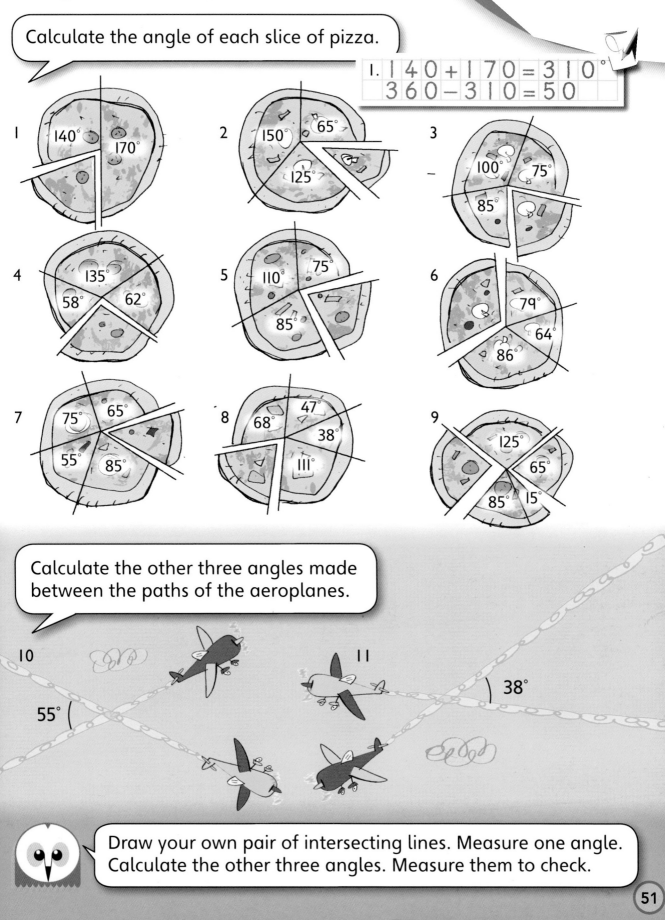

1 140° 170°

2 150° 65° 125°

3 100° 75° 85°

4 135° 58° 62°

5 110° 75° 85°

6 79° 64° 86°

7 75° 65° 55° 85°

8 68° 47° 38° 111°

9 125° 65° 85° 15°

Calculate the other three angles made between the paths of the aeroplanes.

10 55°

11 38°

Draw your own pair of intersecting lines. Measure one angle. Calculate the other three angles. Measure them to check.

Angles at a point

Write the smaller angle between the hands of each clock or watch. Write your answer to the nearest 10°.

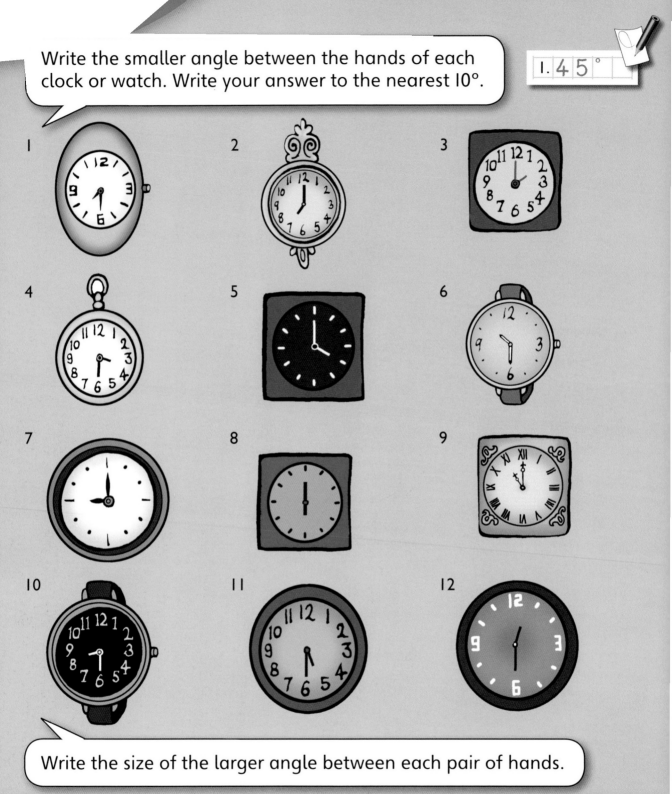

Write the size of the larger angle between each pair of hands.

 Write some different times when the smallest angle between the hands is 105°.

Angles in a triangle

Use a protractor to measure the size of each angle.

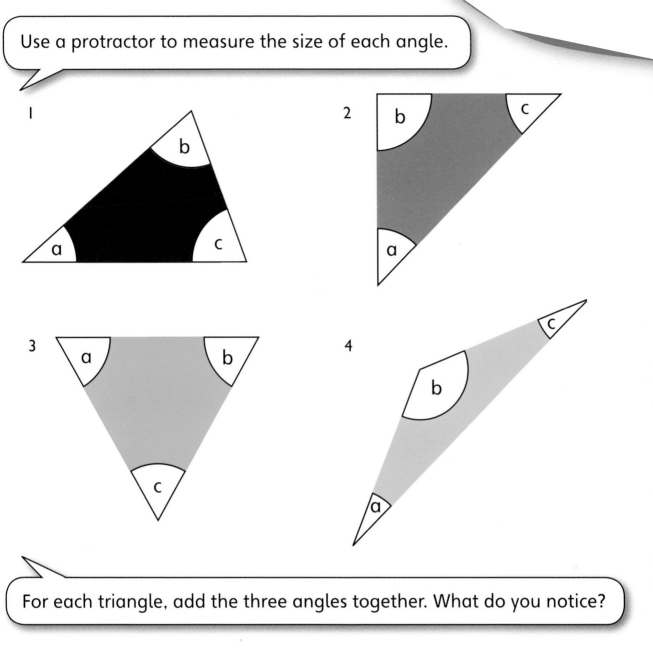

1

2

3

4

For each triangle, add the three angles together. What do you notice?

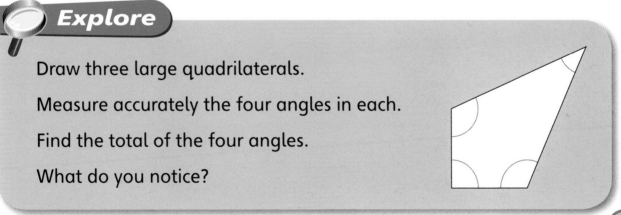

Write the size of the missing angles.

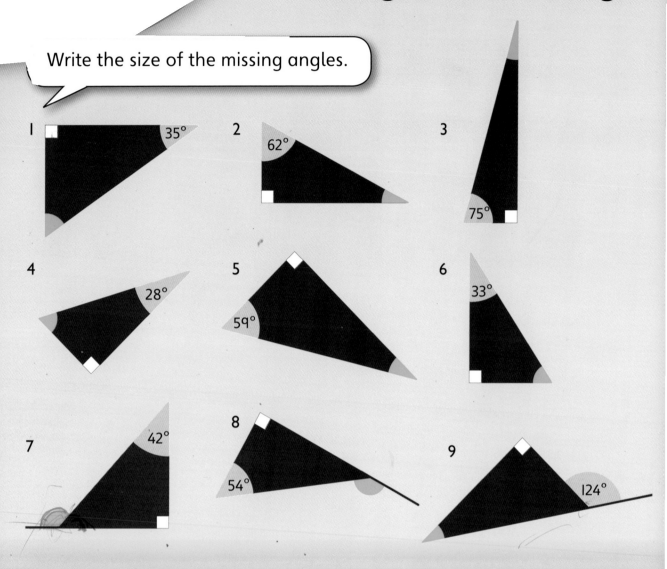

1   35°

2   62°

3   75°

4   28°

5   59°

6   33°

7   42°

8   54°

9   124°

Three angles of a triangle are all multiples of 10°. If one angle is 40°, what could be the sizes of the other two angles?

40°

Investigate how many of these triangles are equilateral, isosceles or right-angled.

Repeat your investigation with one angle being 60°. Is the number of possible triangles the same?

(Hint: an isosceles triangle has two equal angles.)

Angles in a triangle

Write the size of the missing angles.

1
42°
58°

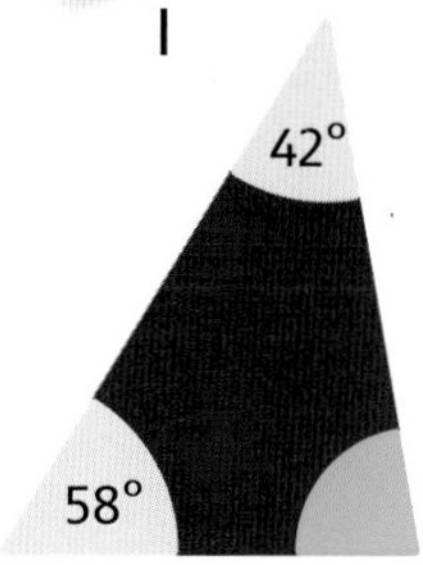

2
85°   61°

3
43°
61°   ___

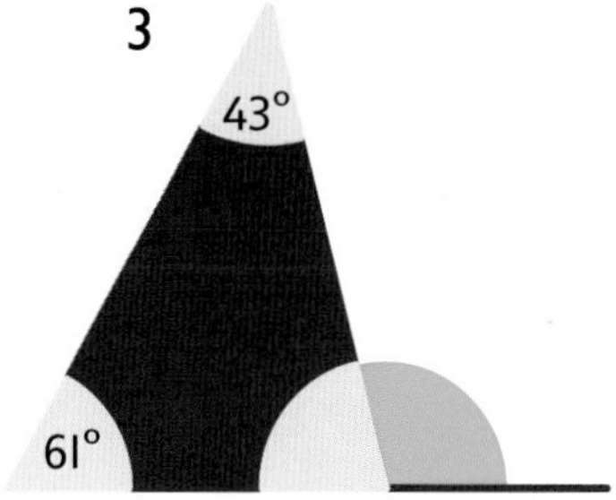

4
36°
73°   ___

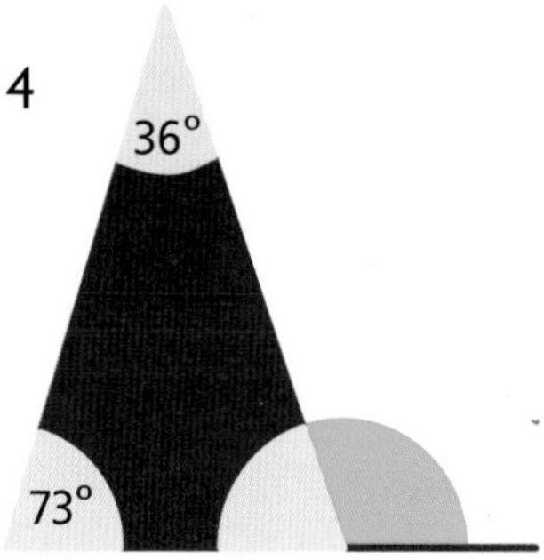

5
37°   41°

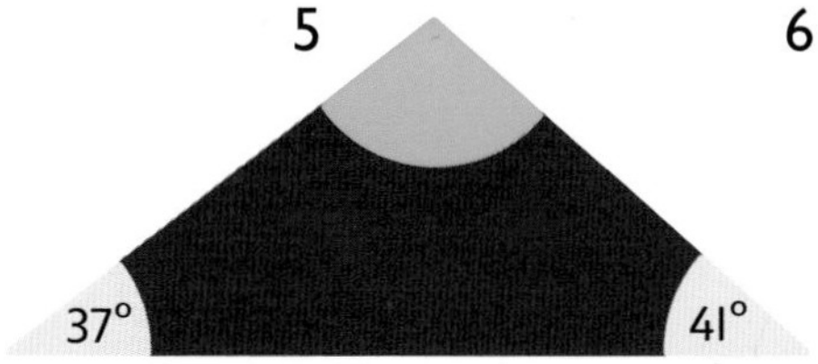

6
___
41°
82°

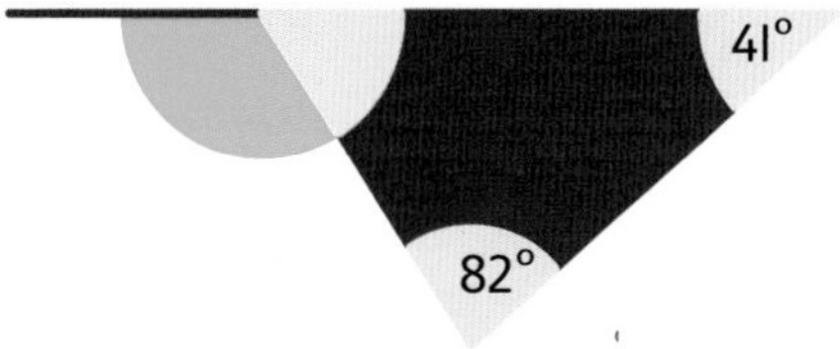

Write the missing angles in these isosceles triangles.

7
38°   a
b

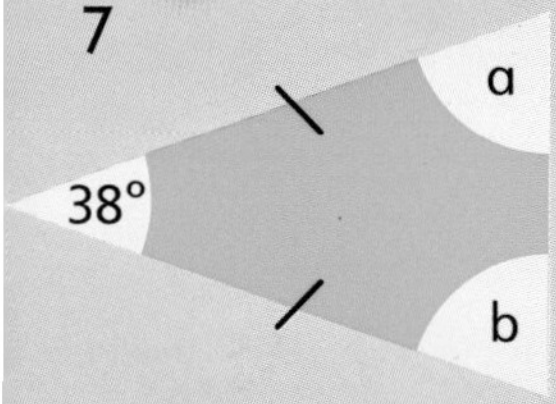

8
a   b   126°
c

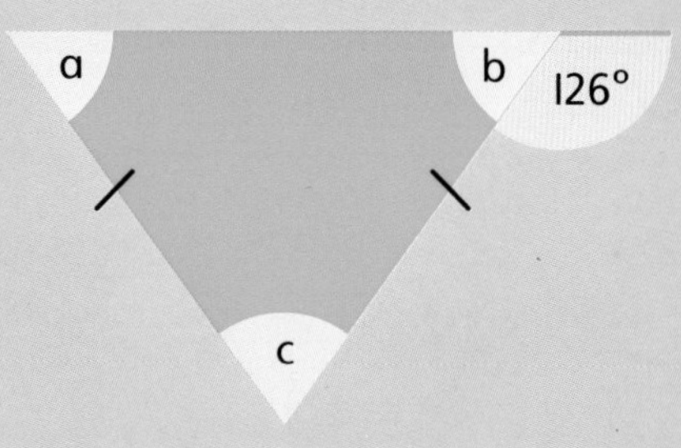

9
134°   a   b
c

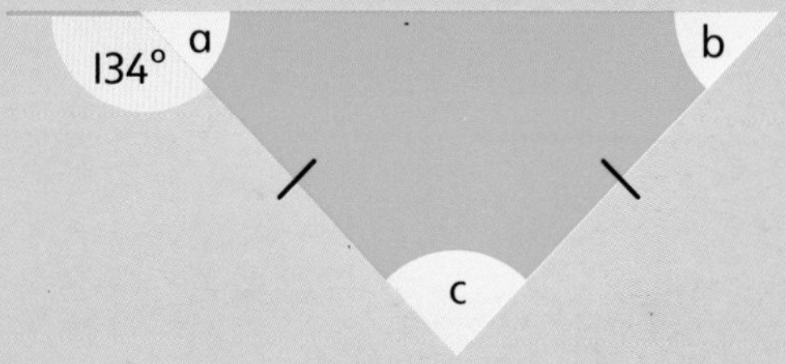

This is one of the angles in an isosceles triangle. Find the others. There are two possible angles for each triangle.

10 48°   11 18°   12 66°   13 83°

There are three angles in a triangle. All three can be multiples of 3°, e.g. 30°, 60°, 90°. Can all three angles be multiples of 4, of 5, of 6? Give examples.

Angles in a triangle

True or false?

1 A right-angled triangle cannot have an obtuse angle.

2 A triangle can be both right-angled and equilateral.

3 A triangle can be both right-angled and isosceles.

4 An isosceles right-angled triangle has an angle of 45°.

5 The angles in an equilateral triangle are all 60°.

6 The total of the angles in a quadrilateral is the same as four right angles.

Explore

Investigate the total of the angles in different polygons by splitting them into triangles.

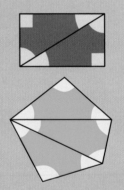

For example, a quadrilateral can be split into two triangles. The angles in a triangle total 180°, the same as two right angles. So the total of the angles in a quadrilateral is four right angles (360°).

Try this with different sized polygons. Record your results in a table.

Number of sides	Total of angles
4	Four right angles (360°)
5	
6	

Calculate the missing angles.

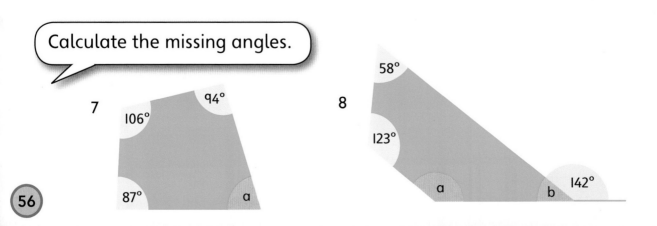

7

106° 94° 87° a

8

58° 123° a b 142°

Adding three and four numbers

Write the total price. How much change do you get from £20?

1. £2 + £8 + £5 + £4 = £19
   £1 change

1

£5   £8   £4   £2

2

£3   £7   £8

3

£3   £9   £4

4

£2   £5   £7   £4

In Nonsense Land there are only £3, £2 and £5 notes.
Are there any amounts up to £20 that you cannot make?

Write the total amount.

5   200   500   800   600   6   500   700   800

7   300   900   600   700   8   400   300   800

9   800   300   500   100   10 600   400   300   500

BANK PLC

£

Write the total amount.

1. £ 4 0 0 + £ 8 0 0 + £ 7 0 0 + £ 5 0 0 + £ 6 0 0 = £ 3 0 0 0

1   £400   £800   £700   £500   £600

2   £500   £900   £300   £700   £800

3   £300   £800   £400

4   £200   £300   £800   £400   £500

5   £100   £700   £900   £300

6   £800   £200   £400   £500

Add four different multiples of 100 to total 1200.
How many ways can you find to do this?

Copy and complete.

7. 4 5 + 3 8 + 2 7 + 3 5 = 1 4 5

7   45 + 38 + 27 + 35   8   37 + 45 + 82 + 38

9   57 + 28 + 32 + 65   10   24 + 29 + 56 + 31

11 27 + 73 + 66 + 42   12   43 + 79 + 21 + 64

Adding and subtracting

Copy and complete.

1. 123 + 100 = 223
123 + 99 = 222

1   123 + 99

2   276 − 98

3   452 + 198

4   807 − 499

5   643 + 103

6   876 − 102

7   5246 + 2997

8   3782 − 1996

9   6130 + 399

10 7423 − 1006

11 2106 − 701

12 4327 + 296

13 6428 − 299

14 4832 + 202

15 8506 − 398

Write an addition of two 3-digit numbers that are both 1 less than a multiple of 100. Repeat this three times. What is the last digit of the answer?

16 James had 786 g of chocolate. He ate 399 g. How much does he have left? Write the answer in kilograms.

17 Sally cycles 3·26 miles to work and then 4·98 home via the shops. How far does she cycle in total?

18 Ilesh has saved £464. He spends £99 on a DVD player, £49 on a CD player and £298 on a computer. How much has he left?

Adding and subtracting

Each child buys a ticket.
How much does each have left?

Tickets!!

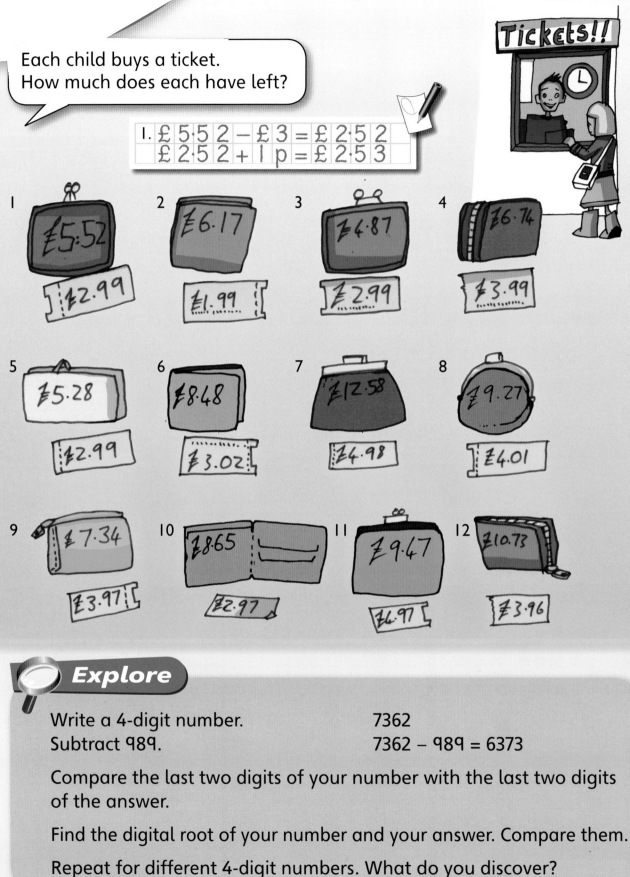

1. £5·52 − £3 = £2·52
   £2·52 + 1p = £2·53

1 £5·52 £2.99

2 £6.17 £1.99

3 £4·87 £2·99

4 £6.74 £3.99

5 £5.28 £2.99

6 £8·48 £3.02

7 £12·58 £4.98

8 £9.27 £4.01

9 £7.34 £3.97

10 £8·65 £2·97

11 £9·47 £4·97

12 £10.73 £3·96

Explore

Write a 4-digit number.   7362
Subtract 989.   7362 − 989 = 6373

Compare the last two digits of your number with the last two digits of the answer.

Find the digital root of your number and your answer. Compare them.

Repeat for different 4-digit numbers. What do you discover?

Subtracting

Write how much to the next £10.

1. £3·46   £4   £10
     54p   £6
£6·54 to go

1   £3·46

2   £15·17

3   £8·34

4   £28·28

5   £16·37

6   £22·64

7   £17·42

8   £6·93

9   £12·45

10   £26·76

11   £14·66

12   £12·58

Copy and complete.

13. £3·86   £4   £5·40
    14p   £1·40   £1·54

13 £5·40 – £3·86 = ☐

14 £7·20 – £4·63 = ☐

15 £6·10 – £3·74 = ☐

16 £8·70 – £5·84 = ☐

17 £6·30 – £2·67 = ☐

18 £7·60 – £3·76 = ☐

19 £5·30 – £2·45 = ☐

20 £4·20 – £1·73 = ☐

21 £8·50 – £4·66 = ☐

22 £8·16 – £4·25 = ☐

Start at £10. Subtract 99p, then 98p, then 97p …
How far can you go? What is left at the end?

Subtracting

What is the difference in height between the two rockets?

1

7·53 m   2·85 m

2

6·14 m   3·46 m

3

8·23 m   2·65 m

4

4·37 m   3·69 m

5

6·75 m   2·84 m

6

5·43 m   3·28 m

7

5·62 m   4·51 m

8

3·86 m   6·74 m

9

8·37 m   2·49 m

Start with a 2-place decimal (e.g. 8·73). Reverse the digits (3·78). Find the difference between the two numbers. Repeat. What do you notice?

Copy and complete.

10. 678   700   1000

      22   300   472   794
   1472 − 678 = 794
   1·472 − 6·78 = 7·94

10 1472 − 678

    14·72 − 6·78

11 2312 − 865

    23·12 − 8·65

12 1414 − 764

    14·14 − 7·64

13 21·38 − 9·45

14 19·54 − 7·63

15 18·37 − 6·54

16 22·76 − 8·84

17 17·25 − 9·36

18 21·68 − 7·79

Subtracting

1

> Choose two places. Work out the difference between their populations, choosing your own method. Repeat for different places: make sure you do all ten calculations.

Netherton 8342 people

Beauville 3676 people

Cotteslowe 6997 people

Rotherthorpe 7368 people

Northfield 5643 people

> Use 0–9 digit cards. Create a subtraction like this:
>
> ☐·☐☐ − ☐·☐☐
>
> Discuss with your partner how best to solve it.

> Copy and complete.
> Choose your own method!

2. $4·45 − 2·68 = 1·77$

2   $4·45 − 2·68$

3   $1·34 − 0·99$

4   $5·67 − 2·34$

5   $3·26 − 1·77$

6   $3·45 − 1·99$

7   $8·12 − 4·8$

8   $7·2 − 5·43$

9   $9·58 − 4·48$

10   $7·01 − 1·82$

11   $7·68 − 5·3$

12   $4·49 − 2·51$

13   $0·6 − 0·32$

Subtracting

1 Chang ordered a pizza for £3·99 and an apple pie for £2·59. How much change does he get from £10? What is the fewest number of coins he could have in change?

2 Willa walked 28·3 miles and then took a train for 46·8 miles. How far has she to go to travel 99 miles?

3 In a leap year Callum studied for 229 days. How many days were leisure days? If he was at home for 296 days, for how many weeks was he on holiday?

Write your own word problem involving subtraction of decimals and using the number 1·89.

Write the number of fish left after the sea-lion has eaten!

4. 3 1 4 — 1 9 8 = 1 1 6 fish

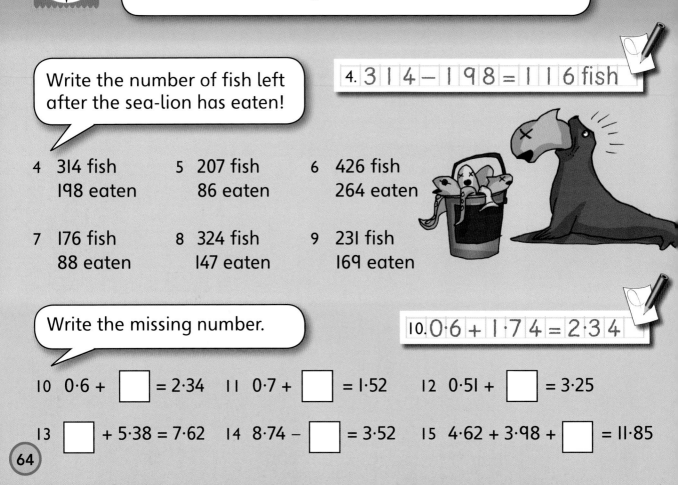

4 314 fish 198 eaten	5 207 fish 86 eaten	6 426 fish 264 eaten
7 176 fish 88 eaten	8 324 fish 147 eaten	9 231 fish 169 eaten

Write the missing number.

10. 0·6 + 1·74 = 2·34

10 0·6 + ☐ = 2·34   11 0·7 + ☐ = 1·52   12 0·51 + ☐ = 3·25

13 ☐ + 5·38 = 7·62   14 8·74 − ☐ = 3·52   15 4·62 + 3·98 + ☐ = 11·85

Multiplying and dividing

Write the cost of two of each item.

1. double £43 = £80 + £6 = £86

1. £43
2. £54
3. £72
4. £84
5. £37
6. £29
7. £69
8. £87
9. £78

Half price sale! Write the new cost.

10. half of £48 = £20 + £4 = £24

10. £48
11. £64
12. £78
13. £164
14. £116
15. £152
16. £134
17. £178
18. £196

You have £192 to spend. Write the original price of three items you could buy.

Multiplying and dividing

Draw two large 5 × 4 grids. Follow the instructions to write new numbers in each box.

1. | 3 | 4 | 1 | 5 | 0 |
   |---|---|---|---|---|
   | … | … | … | … | … |

1 Double the numbers:

17	75	34	48	23
42	87	27	16	56
38	36	73	64	88
49	54	82	91	26

2 Halve the numbers:

72	114	48	138	74
126	84	152	96	36
130	172	56	188	102
194	88	166	92	122

Write the number of shoes.

3   240 pairs

4   330 pairs

5   480 pairs

6   640 pairs

7   830 pairs

8   770 pairs

9   590 pairs

10   460 pairs

11   880 pairs

Write the number of pairs of shoes.

12   840 shoes

13   680 shoes

14   870 shoes

15   1250 shoes

16   1490 shoes

17   1530 shoes

18   1770 shoes

19   1390 shoes

20   1180 shoes

A number is halved and doubled. The difference between the two answers is 720. What could the number have been?

Multiplying and dividing

Find the missing number.

1 double ☐ = 3060 2 half of 6800 = ☐ 3 half of ☐ = 240

4 double ☐ = 500 5 half of ☐ = 320 6 double ☐ = 1400

Explore

Use 1–9 digit cards and two 0 cards.
Make pairs of numbers, one 3-digit and one 4-digit,
each ending in 0. One number must be double the other:

6 7 0   1 3 4 0

Investigate different pairs you can make.

Check each answer. If the answer is correct,
double it. If it is incorrect, halve it.

7	2900	8	3700	9	8250	10	4436
	+ 1600		+ 4800		+ 9450		+ 4764
	4700		8500		16700		9700

11	4540	12	6803	13	6370	14	6806
	+ 2960		+ 4797		+ 1430		+ 5804
	7800		11500		7700		12700

Invent one correct and one incorrect addition
that when doubled or halved equals 8700.

Multiplying and dividing

At these football matches, half of the people bought a programme for £4. How many programmes were sold? How much money was raised?

1. 1900 programmes
   £7600

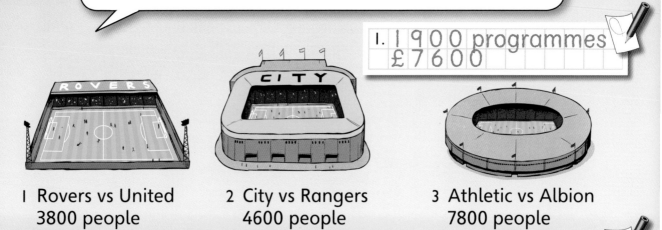

1 Rovers vs United
3800 people

2 City vs Rangers
4600 people

3 Athletic vs Albion
7800 people

Each plank of wood is cut in half. Write the new length.

4. 1·9 m

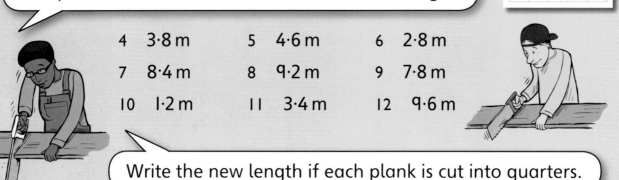

4	3·8 m	5	4·6 m	6	2·8 m
7	8·4 m	8	9·2 m	9	7·8 m
10	1·2 m	11	3·4 m	12	9·6 m

Write the new length if each plank is cut into quarters.

Write the larger of each pair.

13 double 3·6   half of 15·6   14 half of 9·4   double 2·3
15 half of 17·2 double 4·4   16 double 4·7   half of 19·6
17 double 3·7   half of 13·8   18 half of 11·4 double 2·9

Write the difference between each pair.

Create some pairs like this that have a difference of 0·6.

Multiplying by 50 and 25

There are 50 paperclips in a box. How many paperclips in:

1. $13 \times 100 = 1300$
   $13 \times 50 = 650$

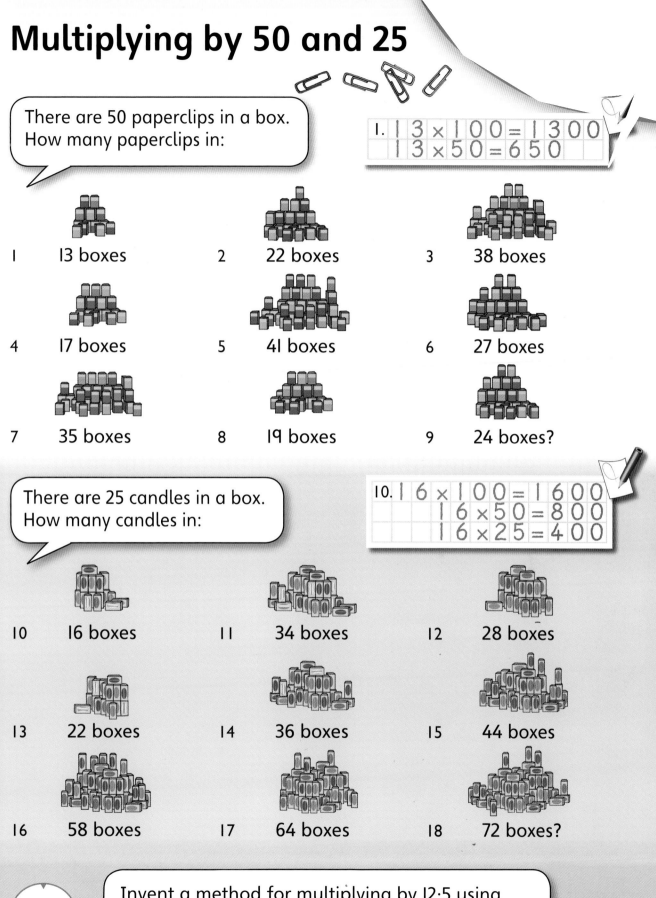

1   13 boxes
2   22 boxes
3   38 boxes

4   17 boxes
5   41 boxes
6   27 boxes

7   35 boxes
8   19 boxes
9   24 boxes?

There are 25 candles in a box. How many candles in:

10. $16 \times 100 = 1600$
    $16 \times 50 = 800$
    $16 \times 25 = 400$

10   16 boxes
11   34 boxes
12   28 boxes

13   22 boxes
14   36 boxes
15   44 boxes

16   58 boxes
17   64 boxes
18   72 boxes?

Invent a method for multiplying by 12·5 using doubling and halving. Write some multiplications by 12·5 for your partner to answer.

Use the machine to help you multiply each pair of numbers.

1. $14 \times 35 = 7 \times 70 = 490$

1	14	35	2	12	15	3	16	25
4	18	25	5	16	30	6	35	18
7	45	12	8	40	18	9	15	16

Explore

Try this method for making multiplications easier.

Halve both numbers.	$22 \times 14 \longrightarrow 11 \times 7$
Multiply them together.	$11 \times 7 = 77$
Double the answer twice.	$154 \longrightarrow 308$

Which multiplications does this make easier?
Try some more. Use a different method from your partner.
Who can get to the answer fastest?

Calculate the area of these pictures.
Double one side and halve the other.

10. $A = 15 \times 14 = 30 \times 7 = 210 \, cm^2$

10. 15 cm
14 cm

11. 16 cm
25 cm

12. 18 cm
45 cm

13. 14 cm
25 cm

14. 55 cm
12 cm

15. 12 cm
35 cm

Use facts to find other facts

1   Write the first ten multiples of 6. Use doubling to write the first ten multiples of 12. Use doubling again to write the first ten multiples of 24. Use the tables to complete these multiplications.

2   3 × 24

3   7 × 24

4   9 × 24

5   6 × 24

6   8 × 24

7   4 × 24

These facts have been obtained by doubling.

1 × 13 = 13

2 × 13 = 26

4 × 13 = 52

8 × 13 = 104

16 × 13 = 208

1 × 16 = 16

2 × 16 = 32

4 × 16 = 64

8 × 16 = 128

16 × 16 = 256

1 × 15 = 15

2 × 15 = 30

4 × 15 = 60

8 × 15 = 120

16 × 15 = 240

Use the facts above to complete these multiplications.

8   3 × 13

9   12 × 16

10   5 × 13

11   3 × 15

12   7 × 13

13   21 × 16

14   11 × 13

15   5 × 15

16   11 × 16

17   17 × 15

18   17 × 13

19   16 × 17

20   13 × 13

21   6 × 15

22   16 × 25

23   24 × 13

24   18 × 13

25   13 × 15

26   31 × 13

27   11 × 15

Use doubling to create a table for ×17 facts.
Use it to write at least five other really hard ×17 facts!

71

14 × 15 = 210

16 × 24 = 384

36 × 25 = 900

48 × 30 = 1440

35 × 44 = 1540

Use the multiplications to help you complete these.

1. 14 × 15 = 210
   7 × 15 = 105

1	7 × 15	2	22 × 35	3	8 × 48	4	24 × 30
5	48 × 15	6	35 × 88	7	32 × 24	8	30 × 96
9	60 × 48	10	72 × 25	11	24 × 60	12	28 × 15
13	22 × 70	14	48 × 16	15	96 × 60	16	18 × 50

Use the 16 × 24 fact to help you write the ×48 multiplication table. Can you use it to write the ×32 table?

Use each of these facts to help you write four related facts.

17. 4 × 18 = 72
    4 × 36 = 144
    ...

17	8 × 18 = 144	18	6 × 16 = 96
19	14 × 12 = 168	20	24 × 14 = 336
21	12 × 32 = 384	22	24 × 36 = 864

Mixed numbers and improper fractions

Write the number of bars of chocolate.

1. $2\frac{5}{6}$

1

2

3

4

5

6

7

8

9

Write the number of:

thirds

10 $2\frac{1}{3}$ 11 $3\frac{1}{3}$ 12 $5\frac{2}{3}$

quarters

13 $4\frac{1}{4}$ 14 $1\frac{3}{4}$ 15 $7\frac{2}{4}$

fifths

16 $6\frac{4}{5}$ 17 $4\frac{3}{5}$ 18 $5\frac{2}{5}$

tenths

19 $1\frac{3}{10}$ 20 $3\frac{1}{10}$ 21 $2\frac{7}{10}$

sixths

22 $1\frac{1}{6}$ 23 $1\frac{5}{6}$ 24 $3\frac{5}{6}$

Explore writing, as mixed fractions, the number of hours in 100, 150, 200… minutes. Now try the number of weeks in 10, 20, 30 days.

Mixed numbers and improper fractions

Write the number of teams that can be made from each group of players.

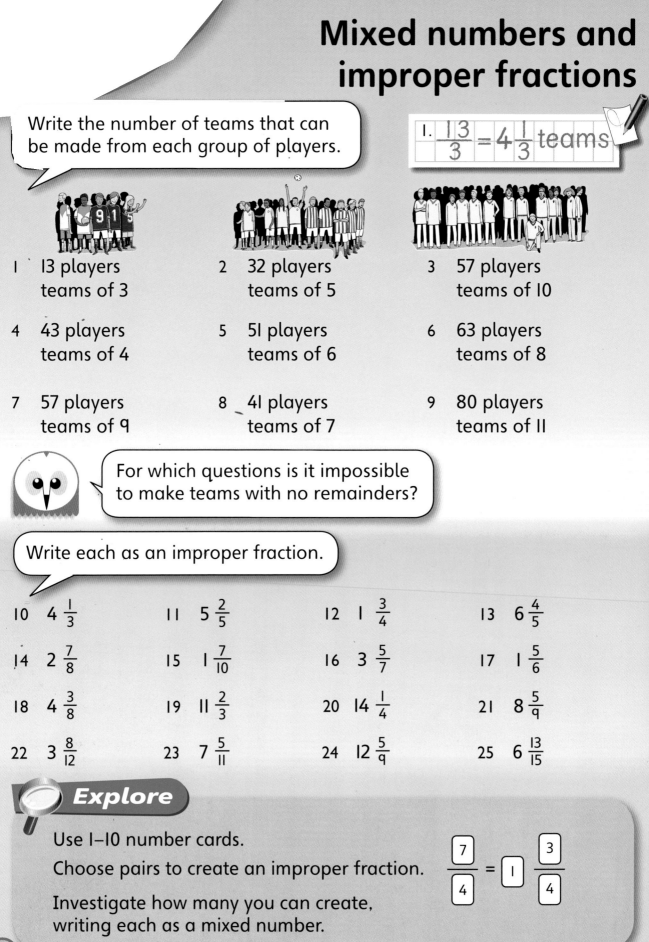

1. 13 players
   teams of 3

2. 32 players
   teams of 5

3. 57 players
   teams of 10

4. 43 players
   teams of 4

5. 51 players
   teams of 6

6. 63 players
   teams of 8

7. 57 players
   teams of 9

8. 41 players
   teams of 7

9. 80 players
   teams of 11

For which questions is it impossible to make teams with no remainders?

Write each as an improper fraction.

10. $4\frac{1}{3}$

11. $5\frac{2}{5}$

12. $1\frac{3}{4}$

13. $6\frac{4}{5}$

14. $2\frac{7}{8}$

15. $1\frac{7}{10}$

16. $3\frac{5}{7}$

17. $1\frac{5}{6}$

18. $4\frac{3}{8}$

19. $11\frac{2}{3}$

20. $14\frac{1}{4}$

21. $8\frac{5}{9}$

22. $3\frac{8}{12}$

23. $7\frac{5}{11}$

24. $12\frac{5}{9}$

25. $6\frac{13}{15}$

Explore

Use 1–10 number cards.

Choose pairs to create an improper fraction.

$\frac{7}{4} = 1\frac{3}{4}$

Investigate how many you can create, writing each as a mixed number.

Mixed numbers and improper fractions

Write each division as a mixed number.

1. $41 \div 5$
2. $28 \div 3$
3. $19 \div 4$

4. $32 \div 7$
5. $57 \div 5$
6. $71 \div 6$

7. $44 \div 6$
8. $67 \div 7$
9. $53 \div 6$

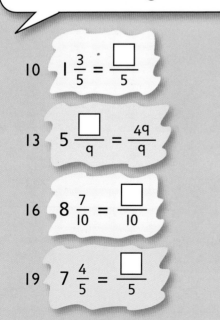

Explore

Choose any odd number between 10 and 40, e.g. 31.

Divide the number by 2. $15\frac{1}{2}$

Then divide the number by 3. $10\frac{1}{3}$

Continue up to dividing by 10. Are any divisions exact?

Repeat for different numbers.

Write the missing numbers.

10. $1\frac{3}{5} = \frac{\square}{5}$

11. $2\frac{\square}{7} = \frac{18}{7}$

12. $3\frac{2}{3} = \frac{\square}{3}$

13. $5\frac{\square}{9} = \frac{49}{9}$

14. $\square\frac{3}{8} = \frac{51}{8}$

15. $\square\frac{3}{4} = \frac{19}{4}$

16. $8\frac{7}{10} = \frac{\square}{10}$

17. $2\frac{\square}{6} = \frac{17}{6}$

18. $\square\frac{1}{2} = \frac{9}{2}$

19. $7\frac{4}{5} = \frac{\square}{5}$

20. $5\frac{\square}{3} = \frac{17}{3}$

21. $\square\frac{2}{15} = \frac{47}{15}$

$$1. \quad 3\frac{3}{4} = \frac{15}{4} = \frac{30}{8}$$

Copy and complete

1 $3\frac{3}{4} = \frac{}{8}$

2 $4\frac{2}{3} = \frac{}{6}$

3 $5\frac{1}{2} = \frac{}{8}$

4 $3\frac{2}{5} = \frac{}{10}$

5 $4\frac{5}{6} = \frac{}{12}$

6 $3\frac{1}{3} = \frac{}{9}$

7 $2\frac{1}{4} = \frac{}{12}$

8 $5\frac{3}{8} = \frac{}{16}$

9 $1\frac{4}{5} = \frac{}{20}$

10 $4\frac{3}{4} = \frac{}{20}$

11 $2\frac{}{5} = \frac{24}{10}$

12 $3\frac{}{7} = \frac{50}{14}$

Who am I? I can be more than one number!

13 I am a mixed number between 3 and 5. The numerator and denominator of my fraction part have a total of 6.

14 I am an improper fraction whose numerator and denominator are both odd and total 10.

15 I am a mixed number. The total of the digits for my whole number part, my numerator and my denominator is 9.

Explore

Use 1–8 number cards.

Use sets of three cards to make mixed numbers.

$4\frac{1}{5}$

Investigate how many different mixed numbers you can create between 5 and 7.

Can you write them in order?

Equivalent fractions

Write these fractions in their simplest form.

1. $\dfrac{9}{12} = \dfrac{3}{4}$

1 $\dfrac{9}{12}$

2 $\dfrac{8}{10}$

3 $\dfrac{6}{9}$

4 $\dfrac{12}{18}$

5 $\dfrac{15}{40}$

6 $\dfrac{20}{24}$

7 $\dfrac{18}{30}$

8 $\dfrac{21}{28}$

9 $\dfrac{14}{42}$

10 $\dfrac{36}{100}$

11 $\dfrac{24}{50}$

12 $\dfrac{49}{63}$

Copy and complete.

13 $\dfrac{\square}{5} = \dfrac{6}{10}$

14 $\dfrac{4}{7} = \dfrac{\square}{21}$

15 $\dfrac{5}{\square} = \dfrac{20}{36}$

16 $\dfrac{2}{3} = \dfrac{16}{\square}$

17 $\dfrac{15}{40} = \dfrac{\square}{8}$

18 $\dfrac{\square}{42} = \dfrac{5}{6}$

19 $\dfrac{1}{9} = \dfrac{8}{\square}$

20 $\dfrac{7}{\square} = \dfrac{28}{20}$

21 $\dfrac{\square}{3} = \dfrac{28}{21}$

22 $\dfrac{21}{\square} = \dfrac{3}{4}$

23 $\dfrac{25}{45} = \dfrac{5}{\square}$

24 $\dfrac{7}{8} = \dfrac{\square}{48}$

Create some pairs of equivalent fractions that have a missing number. Challenge your partner to solve them.

Write each set of fractions in order, smallest first. Draw your own fraction lines to help you.

1   $\frac{5}{6}$, $\frac{5}{12}$

2   $\frac{2}{3}$, $\frac{3}{5}$

3   $\frac{5}{6}$, $\frac{7}{8}$

4   $\frac{5}{12}$, $\frac{5}{6}$, $\frac{3}{4}$

5   $\frac{7}{15}$, $\frac{1}{2}$, $\frac{4}{5}$

6   $\frac{1}{7}$, $\frac{2}{3}$, $\frac{2}{21}$

7   $\frac{4}{9}$, $\frac{5}{18}$, $\frac{1}{2}$

8   $\frac{7}{10}$, $\frac{3}{5}$, $\frac{1}{2}$

9   $\frac{7}{12}$, $\frac{19}{24}$, $\frac{5}{6}$

10   $\frac{17}{30}$, $\frac{4}{5}$, $\frac{1}{3}$

11   $\frac{15}{24}$, $\frac{3}{8}$, $\frac{2}{3}$

12   $\frac{1}{5}$, $\frac{27}{30}$, $\frac{5}{6}$

Cho has 12 marbles. She shares them between three friends, giving $\frac{1}{2}$ to one friend, $\frac{1}{6}$ to another and $\frac{1}{4}$ to the other. What other fractions could she use to share the marbles?

True or false?

13   Ten thirtieths is double one sixth.

14   $\frac{2}{7}$ is half of $\frac{20}{35}$

15   One half is one fifth more than three tenths.

16   $\frac{16}{40} = \frac{3}{5}$

17   Double one fifth is half of eight tenths.

18   One half of ten sixtieths is half of one twelfth.

19   $\frac{3}{7} + \frac{2}{5}$ is $\frac{58}{70}$

Ordering fractions

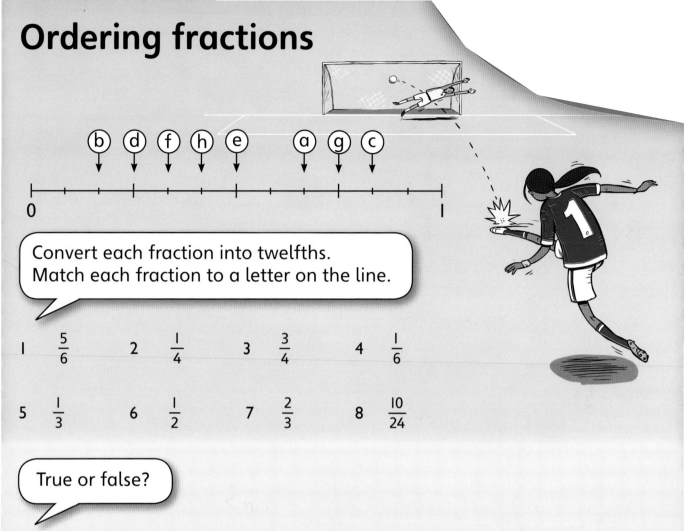

Convert each fraction into twelfths.
Match each fraction to a letter on the line.

1 $\frac{5}{6}$ 2 $\frac{1}{4}$ 3 $\frac{3}{4}$ 4 $\frac{1}{6}$

5 $\frac{1}{3}$ 6 $\frac{1}{2}$ 7 $\frac{2}{3}$ 8 $\frac{10}{24}$

True or false?

9 One half is less than four sevenths.

10 One quarter is the same as three twelfths.

11 Five twentieths is greater than one fifth.

12 One third is equal to two sixths and also to four twelfths.

13 $\frac{1}{2} > \frac{7}{15}$ 14 $\frac{5}{6} = \frac{25}{30}$ 15 $\frac{1}{2} = \frac{2}{8}$

16 $\frac{2}{5} > \frac{2}{7}$ 17 $\frac{4}{5} = \frac{28}{35}$

Write three fractions where the first is half of the second and the second is half of the third. Work with a partner to write three sets like this.

Number line: 0, $\frac{5}{30}$, $\frac{10}{30}$, $\frac{15}{30}$, $\frac{20}{30}$, $\frac{25}{30}$, 1

Use the fraction line. Convert each fraction into 30ths. Write each set of fractions in order, smallest first.

1. $\frac{1}{2} = \frac{15}{30}$, $\frac{1}{3} = \frac{10}{30}$, $\frac{2}{5} = \frac{12}{30}$
$$\frac{1}{3}, \frac{2}{5}, \frac{1}{2}$$

1 $\frac{1}{2}$, $\frac{1}{3}$, $\frac{2}{5}$

2 $\frac{2}{3}$, $\frac{3}{5}$, $\frac{7}{10}$ 3 $\frac{3}{5}$, $\frac{1}{2}$, $\frac{5}{6}$ 4 $\frac{13}{15}$, $\frac{4}{5}$, $\frac{7}{10}$

5 $\frac{8}{10}$, $\frac{2}{3}$, $\frac{4}{5}$ 6 $\frac{3}{15}$, $\frac{3}{5}$, $\frac{1}{2}$ 7 $\frac{12}{60}$, $\frac{2}{15}$, $\frac{4}{6}$

Convert each fraction using the suggested denominator. Write < or > between the fractions.

8. $\frac{1}{2} = \frac{7}{14}$, $\frac{4}{7} = \frac{8}{14}$
$$\frac{1}{2} < \frac{4}{7}$$

8 $\frac{1}{2}$, $\frac{4}{7}$ 14ths   9 $\frac{2}{3}$, $\frac{5}{8}$ 24ths

10 $\frac{2}{5}$, $\frac{1}{4}$ 20ths   11 $\frac{5}{6}$, $\frac{2}{3}$ 6ths

12 $\frac{2}{3}$, $\frac{3}{4}$ 12ths   13 $\frac{7}{9}$, $\frac{1}{2}$ 18ths

14 $\frac{2}{5}$, $\frac{1}{3}$ 15ths   15 $\frac{3}{4}$, $\frac{1}{2}$, $\frac{7}{8}$ 8ths

Work with a partner. Write a different fraction each, with a numerator of 1. Work out some fractions that lie between your two fractions.